A JOURNEY TO

HELL

HEAVEN

AND

BACK

FOREWORD BY SID ROTH

A JOURNEY TO
HELL
HEAVEN
AND
BACK

IVAN TUTTLE

It's Supernatural! Press and Messianic Vision Inc.

Cover and interior by Terry Clifton

ISBN 13 TP: 978-0-7684-5835-0
ISBN 13 eBook: 978-0-7684-5836-7
ISBN 13 HC: 978-0-7684-5838-1
ISBN 13 LP: 978-0-7684-5837-4

For Worldwide Distribution, Printed in the U.S.A.
1 2 3 4 5 6 7 8 / 24 23 22 21 20

DEDICATION

I would like to dedicate this book to two very special people in my life—my mother, Helen, and my son, Christopher.

My mother Helen, because without her I would still be in hell forever, being tortured for all eternity. Thank you, Mother, for your prayers. My mother has prayed for me more than 40,000 times in her lifetime. She has graduated to Heaven now, and I know exactly where she's spending her eternity!

My son Christopher, because he has been the recipient of the gifts God has given me and has grown into a fine man of God. He is the greatest son a father could ever have. Thank you, Son, for everything!

CONTENTS

FOREWORD

I FIRST MET IVAN TUTTLE WHEN HE WAS A guest on one of the many shows we produce for our two television networks. Right away, I knew he was someone I wanted to interview on our anchor show, *It's Supernatural!* Then, as I found out more about him, I knew we had to publish his book through our It's Supernatural! Press. We only publish a limited number of books, but they are ones that have the handprint of God to impact His Kingdom.

The revelation of heaven and hell that Ivan received in 1978 was so profound that God told him not to even talk about it for 35 years! Even his wife did not know the story. And even after 35 years, he still could not include portions of this revelation in the first edition of his book. Now this expanded, updated edition includes details never revealed before. God told Ivan the delay was because he was was not ready, and the world was not ready to receive this revelation.

This is God's time now. What you are holding in your hands has the power to change your life. And if you're lukewarm and have been "dumbed down" in your spirit by religious or seeker-sensitive Christianity, get ready to have your world rocked!

Even after all these years, Ivan is still discovering new revelation from heaven that was downloaded to him during his original trip. Many of my guests who have visited heaven find they received a lifetime of information that is brought to remembrance at the right time.

This might surprise you, but my favorite part of the book is where Ivan talks about the creation of the earth. The love God has for humanity was so clearly displayed.

This new season on earth—defined by the Greater Glory—is the ONLY generation in which I would want to be born. We are about to see demonstrations of God's miracles like the world has never seen and a billion-soul harvest. Yes, there will be challenging times ahead, but if you live in His Glory 24/7, it won't matter.

I see this book as essential information that will cause you to be normal—that's normal as defined by the Bible. Then you will be in position to fulfill your God-given destiny. In a short season, you will supernaturally accomplish more than previous generations thought possible.

I know this is the right time for you to read this book. God is about to make up for all the wasted years. The best time in your life is about to happen! Enjoy! As Mordecai told Queen Esther, *"Who knows if you have come to the Kingdom for such a time as this?"* (Esther 4:14 NKJV).

Shalom and Global Glory,

SID ISRAEL ROTH
Host, *It's Supernatural!* Television

INTRODUCTION

THIS BOOK WAS WRITTEN ABOUT THE death, or what society calls an NDE (Near Death Experience), I had back in 1978. At that time in my life, I was not living a very good life; at 26 years old I was mixed up in drugs and my life was spiraling out of control. I made some bad choices for my life back then, but little did I know that my mother would be so instrumental in helping me back.

I went straight to hell when I died. It was a horrible place with people screaming and yelling constantly and begging to get out.

Some people had been there for thousands of years, and they would beg everyone new being brought into hell, asking them to help them get out. Hell was the most horrible place I had ever seen, and since that experience I plan on staying out. There are monsters or demons in hell, and what they do to you is unbelievable. You will find out more about them and what hell is like as you read this book.

After being in hell for a little time, I was taken to heaven because of a special promise, which I will disclose later. While in heaven, I was met by an angel of God and was told and shown many things about the future and about heaven. There are things about heaven I never knew till going there, and only people who have gone there before can fully understand. I have had the pleasure of meeting a couple other people who have died and gone to heaven, and it is such a pleasure talking with them. It is an experience that very few ever have, and I thank God every day for that chance to visit and come back, but I wish I never had to leave. You will read about many of these experiences in this book.

In this book, I write about my life at the time this experience happened because I want you to know how I was living, why this experience happened like it did, and the reason I was spared and allowed to live and come back to life on earth. It is important that you know what it was like for me as a child growing up, the hardships I went through, and the relationship I had with my father. Understanding how I grew up and how I ended up dead is very important to understanding why I titled the book *Journey to Hell, Heaven, and Back.*

After I came back to life, I was afraid to go back to sleep at first because my mind could not comprehend what my spirit had just gone through. The next morning after dying, I went straight to my doctor's consultation office because I needed to know what had happened to me. I was rather rattled at first, but as my mind started catching up with what happened to my spirit, I began to calm down and started understanding what happened to me.

Back in 1978, I didn't start writing about what happened to me after I died because I was not ready to do that at that point in my life. I was also told by an angel in heaven that I would be told when to write it. At the end of August 2013, the Holy Spirit spoke to me that now it was time to write and tell about my experiences in hell and heaven.

I had never written a book before and had no idea how to write one. I have ADHD and sitting still long enough to write a book seemed impossible, but I did what I was told to do. I can remember so well the day I started writing—I sat down at one end of the sofa and my wife was on the other end, because we have the kind of sofa that has a recliner at each end. I opened up my laptop and began to type. That alone is a sight to see because I have to look at my hands to type; I was never given lessons. I started typing away, and what I thought took only about half an hour ended up being a little over four hours.

As I finished the first eight pages that day, I thought that I was done doing what I was supposed to do. Yes, it was only eight pages, but I had never written that many pages in my life about anything I had ever done or gone through. I was so proud of those eight pages. I sent it to several friends and asked them what they thought, and thank God I have friends who tell the truth! Every one of them told me that there were no details in it and questioned me as to why I didn't give details. Well, that started me on the path of writing this book, and I figured out that those eight pages would be the rough draft outline of my book.

Because I had never written a book before, I went to the one person I knew who has written several books. He is a gracious man and met with me and told me how a book should be laid out and about how many words a book should have in order to be a good book. Now let me explain—I only had about 6,000 words so far, and when he told me my book should have at least 25,000 words in it, my heart sank. I realized then that I had a lot of work to do!

I came home that afternoon and began to write day after day until I knew that the book was complete and that I had included everything the angel in heaven told me I should have in this book. A lot of the things I saw, heard, felt, and experienced are included here, but there is not enough time to disclose everything. However, I hope you enjoy reading it and I pray that this book will *change your life as you know it now.*

Chapter 1

Denial

IT WAS FEBRUARY 1978, AND GRAND RAPIDS, Michigan was very cold. There seemed to be an unusual amount of snow that month. We'd just experienced one of the worst winter snow storms in Grand Rapids' history only a few weeks earlier, and it seemed like the snow just wasn't going to let up. I was working selling Oldsmobiles and Hondas at a car dealership there in Michigan.

It was Thursday, and I couldn't wait to get off of work and head to the bars, but first I needed to go home and smoke a joint. I remember being restless that night because my left leg was bothering me. I thought it was just tight, or maybe I had pulled a calf muscle, so I tried stretching it out. About 8:30 p.m. I headed to the nightclub. I found a few ladies to dance with, but by 11:00 my leg was throbbing so badly that I sat down and didn't dance anymore. I left around midnight—two hours earlier than usual and by myself.

Friday morning around 7:30 a.m., I woke up to more pain in my left calf. I wondered when the muscle cramp was ever going to relax so that it didn't hurt so badly! Even though I was in a lot of pain, I decided to go in to work because I needed a few more sales so I could have more party money for the next few weeks. But my leg was hurting so badly that I couldn't make a sale. As the pain became more intense, I finally left work to go home and lie down with my feet elevated; my leg felt better in that position.

That evening, I went back to the nightclub with some friends. But no matter how stoned I got that night, my leg was killing me, and I wasn't much fun. I declined dancing with any of the ladies who asked me to, telling them, "My old football injury is acting up and it's too difficult to dance." I received great sympathy points from the girls that night; several of them bought me drinks and sat at my table talking with me, but it was difficult holding a conversation with them with all the pain in my leg.

I left around midnight and drove straight home. I awoke in severe pain around 7:30 the next morning. *What a horrible day this is going to be*, I thought. That's when I decided it was time to see a doctor, so I took a shower, got dressed, and started calling around to see if there was a doctor available to see me. I finally found one that was open on Saturdays and he told me to come on in.

Around 9:30 a.m., I arrived at the doctor's office and filled out all the required paperwork. The doctor seemed like a nice guy.

"Well, Mr. Tuttle, what seems to be your problem?" the doctor asked while looking at the paperwork I had filled out. Before I could respond, though, he continued, "Oh, I see, you are having Charlie horses or leg cramps in your left calf. How old are you?" he asked.

"I'm 26, almost 27," I answered.

"Well, drop your pants so I can have a look at it," the doctor said. I dropped my pants and the doctor blurted out, "That leg is really swollen!" Then the doctor had me lie flat on my back on his little exam table while he poked at my leg, took measurements of both calves, listened with his stethoscope to something in both legs, and then stood up straight and said, "I think you have thrombophlebitis. It's a blood clot deep within the calf of the leg and it causes swelling like this. How old are you again?" I told him, and he asked me, "Do you smoke a lot of cigarettes?"

I replied, "I smoke a pack or two a day depending on how many customers I have to wait on." The conversation then turned quite serious as the doctor explained to me what could happen if I didn't receive treatment for the thrombophlebitis right away. He even called the hospital for me and told them I would be coming right over; but I had other ideas as I wasn't ready yet to do that.

I left the doctor's office thinking that blood clots were for old people, not someone my age. I thought that maybe if I just elevated my leg for the rest of the weekend it would go away, so I bypassed the hospital and went straight home. There I took a couple of pillows from the bedroom into the living room and propped my leg up on the sofa and sat back and watched TV all day. A young lady I knew named Jennifer came over and helped take care of me that evening.

But the pain continued for several days. One morning a few days later the throbbing woke me up around 5:00 a.m., and it hurt worse than ever before. Every time my heart would beat, it felt like my leg was going to explode. I couldn't fall back to sleep. I still went to work that day, but by lunchtime I knew I had to do something about it, and soon.

CHAPTER 2

BACK TO MY CHILDHOOD

So how had I gotten this far off course in my life and in my walk with the Lord? in You see, when I was a kid around eight years old, I accepted Jesus into my life and got baptized shortly after that. Then when I was ten years old, I received the baptism of the Holy Spirit. All through my preteen and teenage years, I tried to serve the Lord. Back then I was made fun of sometimes because of it, but I did have my friends at church, so that made things better at times.

One of my best friends at church during those years was Nick Tavani. Nick was one of the smartest people I knew, plus he played the piano. Nick became president of our CA (Christ Ambassadors) group; the CA was a group of teenagers from our church in Forestville, Maryland, which was an Assemblies of God church. Nick accepted me, and I guess you could say he didn't judge me the way some other kids did. Oh, he might have thought I was odd, but he still accepted me. I looked up to Nick and his family; they had a great walk with the Lord and Nick was so talented and smart. Nick often helped me understand things in life that I was unaware of in my small world.

You see, my childhood wasn't the best. I had a father who beat me a lot, but I also had a mother who loved me and prayed for me daily. My father was a bricklayer, a big and strong man who worked all the time trying to get ahead in life. He would work as many as three different jobs at the same time to make sure we had food on the table and a roof over our heads. As a bricklayer, he would work his regular eight- to ten-hour days then come home, shower, and go do a side job. Additionally, every Thursday night he would go to the local supermarket and mop their floors. I had three sisters and one brother.

As a kid I would sit in class and watch the teacher as she taught us stuff so slowly that it felt like I was watching paint dry, so I would look out the window of my class and dream about being in the woods across the playground. I would dream about being Davy Crockett or Daniel Boone, but the problem was I was in the classroom. My mind was so active with thought. I have since been diagnosed as ADHD, but back then they didn't know about ADHD so I was just considered a "bad kid."

When the teacher would notice that I was looking out the window and fidgeting around in my chair, she would ask me a question about whatever subject we were doing, and I had no idea what she was talking about. This got me sent to the principal's office a lot. Everything was just too slow for me. I didn't try to be bad; I always tried to do the right thing. I just lost interest in things quickly and wanted to know what's next. I just couldn't help it; I hated school and wanted to go play out in the woods, anything but sit there in class. This behavior was also displayed at home, where the consequences were much worse.

At school, the worst thing that could happen was the principal would use the paddle on me. She had broken a few of them on me before, but she only swatted me three times at the most. At home, it was much worse because my father would beat me with a belt. Remember, he was a big, strong man—a bricklayer. He knew how to swing that belt, and fifteen to twenty lashes was common. Most of my childhood I had welts all over my behind, my legs, and my back, and sometimes the welts would bleed. My father had such anger toward me. (I eventually found out why, and I will explain later in the book.) Some days he would come home from work and if I did not get out before he came home, he would beat me with the belt asking me, "What did you do wrong today? I know you did something, what was it?" I finally got wise to that, and as soon as I saw him take his belt off I made up stuff that I had done wrong just so my dad would stop beating me so much. If I waited until he started beating me, I might get ten or fifteen whacks with the belt and then admit to something and get ten or fifteen more whacks with the belt, but if I just made something up he would only hit me about fifteen to twenty times.

To make matters worse for me as a kid, I had been born with a deformed left hand and arm. So not only did I get abuse from my dad, but at school most of the kids made fun of me and it seemed like someone always wanted to beat me up or start a fight with me after school. I was not a violent kid, but I quickly got tired of kids hitting me and making fun of me, so I stood up to them. I may have been skinny, but I was really strong. I hated fighting because it reminded me of my dad and how it felt to get beaten, so I tried everything to get out of a fight, but when I had no choice

I wasn't going to lose. You see, if I lost a fight and my dad found out about it, he would whip me so hard and tell me I wasn't man enough and other hurtful things like that.

When I was just nine years old, one day right after school on the playground, I punched a kid in a fight so hard it knocked him out. I thought I killed him because his eyes rolled back in his head and he just went down like a limp dish-rag. I was scared and took off running fast. I ran to my house about a half mile away and told my mother what happened, how this kid had started a fight with me and how I hit him, and I thought I killed him. My mother grabbed her keys and we got in the car and she drove as fast as she could back to my school. When we got there the school nurse was just bring-ing this kid around with smelling salts. Thank God I didn't kill him; he was only knocked out. For a few weeks after that fight no kids picked on me because they were afraid that I would knock them out too. Finally, I enjoyed a few weeks of peace in my life—no one to fight and I could walk home without fear.

This bears repeating—I really didn't want to fight and never started a fight in my life. I always made the other person swing at me or hit me first, with just one exception. There was one time I was egged on to starting a fight with a kid from across the street; I sucker punched him and he wouldn't fight. I felt so bad and ran home, up to my room, and started crying. Later that day, I went over to his house and apologized to him and asked for his forgiveness. I couldn't believe that I actually hit a kid for no reason. As far as I was concerned, I was no better than my father after doing that.

During junior high school I did not dress out for PE a lot because I was so embarrassed about the welts all over my back and legs. I didn't want all the other kids thinking I was a bad person, so I hid this very well throughout seventh and eighth grade. Then one day when I was fourteen, I finally stood up to my dad and he quit beating me.

I can remember the day very well. It was a rainy Sunday morning late in November, and I just happened to walk downstairs at the wrong time. My father was upset because there was not enough wood in the wood box by the fireplace for his liking. He was standing in our family room next to the fireplace, so he saw me when I reached the bottom of the steps coming into the room. He said something about getting more wood in the firewood box, but I didn't know he was talking to me. My dad called me over to him and slapped me right across the face and it nearly knocked me out. As I was falling back from the hit, I could hear my father yelling at me about putting some wood in the box.

After I hit the floor and started to regain myself, I told him that I was in my church clothes and asked him if I could get more wood after church. This just upset him all the more that I would try to reason with him; after all, no one ever questioned him. He wanted more pieces of wood in the firewood box right then and there and expected my immediate obedience at his command. Next thing I knew, my dad had picked me up in the air with one hand as he hit me in the chest with his other hand. It knocked the breath out of me and stunned me for a few moments. As I got up this time, I was very mad and had had enough. I shook my fist at my father and said, "You hit me one more time and I will kill you!"

I can picture my father's face right now as it went from anger to laughter. It started with a small little grin, then went to a little bit of a chuckle, and then grew to an all-out hearty laugh. "So you are going to take me on?" my father asked with a huge smile across his face.

I said, "Yes! I am not going to let you keep hitting me like this anymore. I would rather die trying than to allow you to keep hitting me!"

The next thing I knew, he walked away and said, "Go to church." After that, my father never laid a hand on me again.

High school was really different for me. I was rather timid back then and kept mostly to myself, though I did allow a few kids from church to get a little close to me. I became so shy in my high school years that I only talked to a few people in school. I did have a girl-friend, and back in the '60s holding hands was a big deal back and to kiss a girl was about as far as you would ever go out of respect for her and because you knew anything further was wrong. My "puppy love" didn't last long, but it was my first and I have great, clean memories!

Don't get me wrong, I wasn't a perfect kid back then; actually, I was pretty messed up. With all that my father put me through and the harassment from other kids and all the teachers and adults thinking I was a bad kid growing up, I was very insecure. I made a lot of mistakes and never really knew what was the right thing to do in many situations. I was always afraid that I wasn't smart enough to be around anyone my age or older. I believed there was something wrong with me because even my own father rejected me as a child. I didn't find out until my early twenties that I actually have a pretty high IQ of 136.

Because I was pretty much a loner in high school, I used to listen to music a lot. I could sing pretty well but was too shy to get up in front of people by myself. However, I enjoyed singing in the church and the school choir. Even though I was made fun of in high school, I still loved my music. Music was something that I didn't just hear; I felt it, too. I loved music!

After high school I went to a very small Bible college up in Maine. I didn't have the money to attend, but I was accepted anyway, and they allowed me to earn my way through by working for them on their farm. Someone had given the college a dairy farm and the first thing that needed to be done was to clean out the stalls. Wow, that was not fun! But I enjoyed going to college there. I was taught about public speaking by the president of the college. I can remember him calling me out in class and having me say the word "Obadiah." He made me stand up and say it out loud; I had to fill the whole room up with my voice. Now, as I said earlier, I was very shy back then and afraid to speak in public, but I loved the Lord and wanted to preach. Our instructor worked with me and within a few weeks I was over my fear and ready to preach.

This school had connections with churches all over Maine that would allow students to preach. I went to one church outside of Bangor, Maine, and stayed there with the pastor and his wife during a Thanksgiving break. I was there to work for my stay, which meant I got to preach. My first sermon I ever got to preach was on Romans 12:20:

> *If your enemy is hungry, feed him; if he is thirsty, give him something to drink. In doing this, you will heap burning coals on his head.*

This was an old church, and the platform was made of hardwood with no carpeting on it and underneath it was hollow—very hollow. Every step you took on it echoed throughout the building. I was very nervous as I was only eighteen years old and it was my first time being responsible to preach, so I kind of rocked back and forth tapping my feet a lot while I was preaching, and I guess that made more noise than my preaching. I had someone come up to me after the service and tell me next time to try to keep my feet still so they could hear the sermon. I was embarrassed, but it didn't stop me. I loved the Lord so much back then.

Then on one trip home I met a girl who got my attention quick; she was not a Christian, but she was so darn cute. We fell in love, or what I thought was love, within my two-week stay at home, and she begged me not to leave her to go back to college. She convinced me I could make better money doing something other than preaching. She thought I would be perfect for sales and she got me a job at the GEM (Government Employee Membership) store where she worked in the pharmacy. To make a long story short, that is why I left college and that was when I slipped up and walked away from the Lord. Boy, when I make a mistake, I usually make a big one!

CHAPTER 3

BLOOD CLOT

Now back to 1978 and my problem at hand. My health wasn't in the best condition because I would stay up for days on end partying, using different drugs to keep me awake. I knew I had a problem with my left leg that needed to be taken care of, but I hated going to a doctor's office and questioned what was really wrong with my leg. Were they going to operate on it? How would they get the blood clot out, if there was one? The first doctor I went to had wanted me to go to the hospital right away as he thought I had thrombophlebitis—a deep blood clot in the calf of the leg. I didn't take his advice to go to the hospital because I wanted to keep partying—I was young and invincible, right? So I kept up my lifestyle for a few more days until it got so bad that I couldn't walk, sit, or sleep because of the pain and swelling. Finally, I went to the emergency room.

That night they did some tests on me, measured both legs, and believed I had a pretty good-sized blood clot in my left leg and I had to be hospitalized right away. There I was, only 26 years old, and I had something that my grandfather should have. I had nothing but questions: How do they fix this problem? Do they operate on me or what? Finally, a doctor told me that he indeed believed that I had a blood clot in my leg and that it needed to be treated right away or I could die from it. First, they were going to put me in a room and try to stabilize my blood from being so thick, and in order to do that I would need to be off my feet for a few days. Part of the process required them to put me on blood thinners and other medications to thin out my blood and get the swelling down. I thought, *Great, they will fix it in in a day or two and send me back home.* After all, I still had some partying to do. Not so fast.

The doctors checked me into the hospital, but right away there was a problem. I am highly allergic to iodine, the substance used in the IVP dye they needed to inject me with to look at the clot in my leg. There was a new doctor of radioactive treatments at the hospital and he thought of another way to see the blockage. He wanted to do a "radioactive retrograde uptake" on me, something innovative back in 1978. At that time, the ultrasound wasn't perfected enough to look for blood clots in your legs.

They took me into this room where they had this big, round piece of equipment, about three feet in diameter that had two supporting arms holding it up in the air and a table positioned under it. They were able to move this around with ease like a robot. They laid me down on the table beneath this machine and injected my right leg with this radioactive serum and they moved this big round device over my leg as they watched behind some type of monitor. I could see the monitor and all I saw were hundreds of little dots moving up what must have been my leg. Then they injected it into my left leg. This time as I watched the monitor, I didn't see near as many dots going up my leg. The doctors talked amongst themselves and then let me know that I definitely had a blood clot and the best treatment for me was to remain in bed while they thinned my blood out. I needed to wear some kind of stocking type material on my right leg, the one without the clot, in order to equal out the pressure in my legs so my blood would flow better.

They wheeled me into my room, put me in bed, and then put this stocking type thing on my leg, put an IV in me, shot me full of some stuff, and instructed me that I couldn't get out of bed for any reason. There I was, only 26 years old, full of life, Mr. Party Man, and I had to stay in bed. Talk about being depressed. After about an hour lying in bed, I had to use the restroom. I pressed the red little buzzer button and a nurse came into the room and asked, "What can I do for you?" I let her know I had to use the restroom and she said, "Number one or number two?" I about died laughing when she asked me that. I thought, *Do I look like I am five years old*? I told her number two, and she said, "Wait right there, I'll be right back." She came back in the room with a little bedpan, handed it to me with a roll of toilet paper, pulled the curtain around my bed, and said, "Buzz me when you are finished." Right, I am going to do *what* in this pan and then have you come back in this nice-smelling room to take this from me, like it's some kind of *gift* or something?

Needless to say, I had a lot of growing up to do in a very short time. Being in a hospital at 26 and not being able to get out of bed opened me up to a lot of new challenges. I will say that the nurses and volunteers were some of the nicest people I had ever met and were extremely helpful. A couple of them were even downright cute! I went through a lot of embarrassing moments during my stay, like the bedpan issue and then having to get bathed in bed by strangers. I wasn't sure if I was being treated like a baby or like an elderly nursing home patient.

Being a smoker at the time, I needed a cigarette and I couldn't get my friends to come into the hospital to bring me any. Some friends! After about eight hours of no cigarettes I was going crazy, so whenever someone walked past my door, I would ask them if they had any cigarettes. Finally, one guy did, and he brought one into my room. I lit it up and took in a couple of deep drags before the nurse came in my room and read me the riot act about my room being a non-smoking room. Back in the '70s there were smoking and non-smoking rooms in hospitals, restaurants, airplanes, and just about anyplace else that was public. I asked her to please change my room and she argued, "The doctor wanted you in a non-smoking room because he believes smoking causes blood clots."

I begged her to please put me in a smoking room. "I can't get out of bed or anything else and I can't smoke, and you don't want to see me get like I get when I can't have a cigarette!" I really felt like I was in prison at the time—couldn't do this, couldn't do that. I was pleasantly surprised when she came back in my room and told me that she was moving me down the hall to a smoking room!

I was happy. Every day the nurses would come into my room first thing in the morning and check my vital signs, give me a shot of Heparin, a blood thinner, and then within about thirty minutes or so I would get my breakfast—or what was supposed to be breakfast.

Two weeks after I arrived, with no drugs or alcohol for those two weeks, I was finally getting released from the hospital. I couldn't wait to get home and light up a joint. They released me about 4:00 in the afternoon and I got home about 5:00. The first thing I did was light up a joint and smoked it. After that I got something to eat and watched some TV, then smoked some more pot and around 9:00 that night I felt tired and went to bed. My new girlfriend at the time, Jennifer, was staying there with me while I recovered, and she wondered why I was going to bed so early, but for some reason I was exhausted that night and had to go to bed. Usually I stayed up till at least midnight most of the time.

CHAPTER 4

GOING TO HELL

Around 9:20 that night, I was woken up by something or someone grabbing my left wrist and holding on to it very tight, pulling me right up out of my body. I turned around to see my lifeless body just lying there. I was shocked and kept trying to break free from this horrible thing. I even tried to turn the light on in the room to no avail; my hand went right through the wall. This thing had a death grip on my wrist and I could not get free. I looked around at everything in the room just trying to think of a way to escape when all of a sudden we started to move through space and time into this horrible darkness. We moved so fast that time didn't matter, and where it took me was the most horrific place I had ever seen, heard, or smelled. I could hear people screaming; at first the sound was way off in the distance, but within seconds the screams were so loud it was as if they were coming from right beside me. The shrieks were beyond anything I have ever heard before, and the stench was indescribably repulsive. The sense of hopelessness I felt in this place was totally overwhelming.

The realization finally hit me that I was in hell. No, this was not a dream, and it was not a drug-induced hallucination. I was dead and I was in hell. All hope and expectation of life was gone. The evil spirit that had hold of me had begun laughing at me. It was incredibly grotesque looking and had the strength of a hundred men. As I heard the screams and shrieks of the people there, I could feel their pain in a way considerably beyond what we typically feel here on earth. Our earthly minds and bodies cannot begin to understand or exist with that type of pain. The heat there became unbearable, although I didn't ever see actual flames.

Why was I in hell and, I thought, what did I do to deserve this? I was a pretty good kid and I even went to Bible college for a little while. I didn't hurt anyone or kill anybody, so why was I in hell? Then I realized that the answers didn't really matter because I knew there was no escape and I was trapped there forever—and I do mean forever.

At first I didn't realize that I was still moving down toward the center of hell. I wasn't quite there yet; I had only been on the outskirts of hell. All the while, the demon continued to laugh at me with the most hideous sound my ears had ever heard. It was even worse than the deep, echoing demon voices in the movies. As this demon took me deeper into hell, the smell got so terrible that it permeated my whole being, and the sounds of people screaming literally pierced my being. However, I still tried fighting this evil spirit that had me, and I was screaming like the rest of the people there. I could still feel that insufferable heat coming up from below me, too.

Though words seem utterly inadequate in trying to explain this experience, I will try my best to convey to you the hopelessness and horrifying feelings one has when they're in hell. People were all around me. I bumped into some, and they were screaming as loud as they could and cursing God and yelling at me to please tell their children or other loved ones that hell is for real. They knew it was useless, yet they still screamed and cried out in pain. The pain and anguish there is beyond any suffering you have ever known; it literally engulfs your whole being. Kind of like the worst toothache or headache you have ever had times a thousand and it is throughout your whole being. Imagine falling from an airplane at 35,000 feet up and you have no parachute and nothing but concrete below to land on. You know you are going to die. Well, that hopeless feeling you have going all the way down to certain death—that is what hell is like times ten thousand.

There is so much more I could tell you about hell, more ways to try and describe the despair, agony, and suffering, but what it all comes down to is this—just understand, once you are in hell, it is too late to ask God into your life. It's too late to change your ways or to send a message to others about how awful hell really is. Trust me, you are not going to be running around with your pals partying in hell. You are going to be in total darkness and hopelessness with no chance for escape.

This heinous thing that had ahold of me was taking me further down, and as I felt the heat getting hotter I began to scream as loud as I could. I cried out to God but felt it didn't matter. I thought He wouldn't answer my prayers now that I was dead; I'd had that choice while I was alive. Nothing I could do had any meaning now; I was nothing and felt nothing but complete hopelessness. It was dark and frightening. People were still yelling at me as I passed by them. They screamed, "Get me out of here, please!" Most seemed to be locked in place by something unseen; it was too dark for me to tell, but as I moved past them I could see that they could not move. They just grabbed me and tried desperately to hold on to me.

In this state of being, you don't have a body of the type you had when you were alive in your earthly body, but you do have a body. It's difficult to explain in words. You feel pain, and you see and hear everything with perfect vision and hearing. But the pain in hell is unbelievably worse than anything on earth. At least with earthly pain when it gets too bad you can pass out and escape from it, but not in hell. If you get a cut in the flesh, it only hurts where you got cut, but in hell if you cut your finger it hurts throughout your whole being.

I'm sure I have not adequately described the creatures in hell—what they looked like, smelled like, and what they did. There were some creatures that were very big, about ten or twelve feet tall and they were very grotesque with rotted flesh and a smell that matched. Many of them had long, disfigured arms and legs and they were so strong that they could rip you in half. There were others that seemed to just slither around like huge snakes. I could see many of them going to the center of hell and heading back to earth. I assumed they were being instructed on what to do by satan himself and they were returning to earth to do it.

Some of these beasts were creatures of deception; they would go and enter a body in order to possess it. Usually that would be a very pretty woman or handsome man who then would entice someone to have sex with them. These same demonic spirits would also get people to believe in things like fortune telling, horoscopes, mind reading, etc. These evil spirits would actually work in people with these gifts, though in actuality they were really just well-planned guesses as they have had thousands of years to learn all about people. The twists and turns these demon spirits would do to people and the lies they led them to believe were purposefully deceptive.

There are millions of types of demons of numerous sizes, shapes, and assignments, but they all have the same overall mission and that is to destroy your relationship with God any possible way they can. They can come to you in the form of just about anything here on earth, but make no mistake about it, they are here.

People do not realize that many things on earth have demonic beginnings—like stories about vampires, werewolves, white magic, witches, trolls, and ogres. Even the movies where there are supposed to be good witches and warlocks that fight evil come from a demonic background as well. You should also know that video games that have extreme violence, murder, extra lives when you battle evil forces, and the like all have a demonic presence in them. I don't understand why people are so blind to this today, but that, too, is a trick of the devil. There is no doubt in my mind that some people will get this far in my book and stop reading it because it will offend them or they will think I am crazy, and that is what the devil would want so that he can continue to deceive and control people.

Parents, wake up! This happened to me back in 1978 and I was able to see these types of games before they were ever even invented or released. There is no time after you die; it is forever and you are leading your children straight to hell by letting them play these games! Just look back at kids from the '60s and '70s and then look at the kids in the '80s and '90s and you can see the difference. Now look at the kids today—there is very little communication with them, they are always playing these games and ignoring their parents. You go to church and your children do, too, and they seem like good kids, but there is a deep, dark side you do not know about your own children when you allow them access to these things. I understand your kids keep telling you that everyone else does it and so and so allows their kids to do it, but that still doesn't make it alright. Even if the pastor's kids at your church are allowed to play those games or watch those movies it's still opening up a doorway for demonic powers to enter your home and your children.

In hell there was talk about how the demons were going to rob, steal, and destroy parents' relationships with their children. They plan to do it with books, videos, games, music, teachers, and even at times our own government will help. Demons can do things we as humans can't do, so surround your children with prayer on a daily basis. Some of you might think this is strange, but it is so important to pray over your children and plead the blood of Jesus over them, because nothing the devil has ever come up with can penetrate the blood of Jesus! Think of it like this—back when the Israelites were in Egypt and the death angel was sent to kill all of the first born, if you had lamb's blood on your door posts the angel of death could not harm you. Jesus is the Lamb of God and His blood was shed for all of us and by speaking the name of Jesus, pleading the blood of Jesus over your children, you keep the demonic forces from your children. But that is not all you need to do. You need to get rid of those books, CDs, videos and games, etc., or you are inviting the demons back in your house. As parents, you must do your best to keep your children away from those types of entertainment.

One more thing I would like to add—you can't let your guard down as a parent for any reason nowadays. You have to be vigilant. I saw how the demons were using amusement parks and their characters to deceive children to take them into darker places. Children will be sucked into the occult through magic—or what has been called magic—but is just demonic. Waving a magic wand to make something happen is not how God works. Protect your child's mind, heart, soul, and spirit! Children's movies from these places are horrible; they are filled with a demonic theme and presence. Wake Up! Stop thinking it's just make-believe—it's not, it's demonic!

These things I have seen with my own eyes and have experienced firsthand. Hell is real, make no mistake about it, and you are going there unless you ask Jesus into your life. Hell is not something to play with; there I was trapped for all eternity, never to escape. I saw so many people there who never thought they would end up in hell. These were good people—some were even former pastors of churches, deacons, Sunday school teachers, some familiar men and women from our past—very good people, but they were doomed to hell forever. I did not get to ask them how they got there; I was too worried about why I was there and how I was going to handle all this torture and where the demon was taking me.

I heard more screams and more people crying out, and I knew for sure I was going into the pit of hell and that I could never return. I just wish I could get through to you what that felt like. It's kind of like that dream you have when you are just about asleep or just nodded off and all of a sudden you feel like you are falling. Well, it's like that, except you don't wake up and shake it off, you just keep falling and falling and falling. There is no end to it or the torture you are put through—the sounds and the smell. The smell is worse than rotted garbage and the worst sewer odor you could imagine, all combined with the smell of sulfur. I knew then with certainty I was going to just be tortured and burn in hell forever.

I was getting closer to where this demon wanted to take me; I could finally see the devil from a distance. He was not what you might picture him to be; he was actually a bright shining light and was very beautiful, but I could feel the evil that he emitted. I did not see the typically portrayed horns or a long tail, he was actually very good-looking and I think that is why he is able to fool so many people. He only appears to people on earth who are very important to him, so that he can win them over. If he were gross and grotesque like the demons everyone would run from him. So many people have been fooled by him and his lies, including me. I believed the lie that marijuana was good for you because God put it on earth. Well, God may have put it on earth, but not for the purpose we are using it for. He also made cyanide, but if we use it wrong it will kill us. Some things kill the body and those things are bad, but what kills your spirit is even worse.

CHAPTER 5

MORE OF HELL

HERE WERE THINGS IN HELL THAT ARE hard to explain and even harder to describe. Once down there it is very dark, yet you can still see because you are not using your fleshly or earthly eyes but your spiritual ones. People down there seemed to be chained up in little areas, but there were no bars or walls to prohibit them from moving; they just couldn't get out of their assigned areas.

While going through hell I met several people or souls down there as I was moving past them. Some were just everyday ordinary people, just like you and me, and some were mighty people at one time, including preachers. Many people screamed or yelled at me in hell. As soon as I saw these people, in less than a second I knew their stories. The way people communicated in hell was like talking without saying anything, but I heard them clear as a bell. The demonic beast that had a hold of me slowed down so I could hear these stories, and I was allowed to actually talk to several people in hell. Maybe the reason was so I could think, *Now there isn't any hope of ever getting out.* These people didn't seem to deserve hell, so if they couldn't get out, then I had no hope either.

One man's name was Reverend James Wolfe. He was from England, at least 100 or more years ago from what I gathered. James told me that he regretted his sins and he asked me to tell God he was sorry for molesting those little girls. He also regretted cheating people out of food at a local market—he stole food from there and never got caught. He read his Bible every day and prayed for people when asked, but he couldn't stop himself from doing those things. He never thought it mattered that much; no one was hurt, he thought. Now he knows that's not true and that what he did was wrong. He hated hell.

I met a girl named Mary who was only 18 when she died and she couldn't understand why she was in hell. She never really believed in God, heaven, or hell, but she does now. Mary said she was in college and was driving home for Christmas break from college when she got hit head-on by a drunk driver. She couldn't understand why God didn't forgive her because it was not her fault she died before she could accept Christ; it was the drunk's fault.

Mary said she was alive for a few days in a hospital and she could hear her mother and father praying for her, but she could not do anything about it because she could not answer or move. Mary remembered them saying she was brain dead and that the doctors told her mother and father after three days they would take her off of life support if there were no brain waves. Mary could hear all this going on but couldn't do anything about it. Finally, on the third day her mother and father were in her hospital room when the doctor came in and talked with her parents and everyone agreed to disconnect her. This scared Mary because she knew she wasn't dead yet and wanted to stay alive as long as possible—death scared her. Mary watched as her mother and father said goodbye to her and nodded for the nurse in the room to disconnect the life support. From what Mary was saying, I believe she was having an out-of-body experience or NDE. Mary said she couldn't get any air and felt like she was drowning, and she said everything felt stiff like she couldn't move any part of her body. Then this evil spirit came and took her to hell.

One other person allowed to talk to me was a person from Asia, but I am not sure which country. He said his name, but I am not sure how to spell it; it seemed like it was Jung Sho He. He was a jeweler back on earth and he had a wife, two sons, and a daughter. Jung believed there was no God, no heaven or hell, and was shocked when he had a heart attack and died only to find out there was a hell and he was trapped there forever. He begged me to tell his wife and children if I could. At that time, I only knew I was staying there forever like him.

Why were these people telling me these things? Why did they think I could do anything about their situation? This didn't make sense to me at the time. I knew I was lost forever. I knew I blew my only chance to be with God in heaven. Were these people telling me these things to let me know it's hopeless?

The sights in hell are nothing like what has ever been shown to man here on earth. It was worse than any picture or movie I have ever seen. Imagine solid, jagged rock walls with people attached by some invisible force, like being chained up, and these walls go on forever—over a million miles in every direction. It is dark, it stinks—the smell of rotten flesh and garbage mixed with sulfur smell and heat so hot that your flesh would melt off its bones—that is just a little idea of what hell is like. You get there, you don't leave!

Imagine everything I described about hell and then add the torture you go through all the time. You never get a break, not even for a minute. These evil spirits are there to torture you and they get such pleasure out of it. The biggest pleasure they get is when they know you fell for their lie here on earth that they were going to take care of you, that satan was powerful and he would protect you and give you all these wonderful treasures when you die. Yes, they love it when you believe all that. People who believe in Buddha, Muhammad, or other gods—demons laugh at that because those gods were made up by satan himself to satisfy man, to trick them into believing a lie so he could have them forever. They also love those who didn't believe in God while they were living, because when you go to hell it is too late, but you will believe in God then.

Our spirits look a lot like our fleshly bodies—we seem the same way, but different. This is too difficult to explain in our earthly language or too difficult for our brains to comprehend. Not everything in the spirit, in heaven or hell, can be described because it can only be experienced after we leave our earthly bodies behind. With that being said, hell is worse than having someone break every inch of every bone in your body, inch by inch, one bone at a time—slowly so it takes a whole month to do it. Yes, hell is worse than that. The demons are tearing you apart, but you don't come apart; you only rip and tear but you stay together.

This pain is horrible.

I watched as some demons were tearing apart a young lady, maybe 18 to 20 years of age. She was a beautiful young lady at one time, yet these demons have tortured her for over 400 years and they have never stopped. It is not something you can ever get used to; our spirits are not like our earthly brain. We can't reason or rationalize things because we don't need to anymore. This is final.

Imagine having someone tie your hands up to two different car bumpers and your feet at two different car bumpers and then your head tied up to another car bumper. All at once, all the cars start pulling you apart in all different directions, but you never come apart and you can't pass out. You just suffer the pain, over and over again forever and forever. That would be like a vacation in hell, because that's not even close to a minor pain there.

I saw something else that was interesting to me in hell—I saw demons fighting over who gets to torture someone. They seemed to do this a lot, especially over people who claimed to be Christians on earth but hid stuff about their real activities. I call them "fake Christians" because they claim to be a Christian, but their walk with God is nothing like Christ. They were only satisfied with pleasing themselves. That is one of the biggest lies satan has Christians believing—it's okay to want and desire things; it's okay to have an affair, God will forgive you; it's okay to steal, you need the clothes or food; it's okay to cheat on that test, you studied hard and others are cheating; it's okay to spend your money on whatever you like, you don't need to give to the Lord; it's okay to satisfy yourself, everyone does—and the list goes on and on.

The biggest lies are "once saved, always saved" and "extreme grace"! This is spreading at an alarming rate in the world today. These lies are sending more people to hell than atheism. God does forgive you of your sins, but if you keep sinning you don't get a "get out of hell free" card. The Bible says in First Corinthians 6:9-10:

> *Or do you not know that wrongdoers will not inherit the kingdom of God? Do not be deceived: Neither the sexually immoral nor idolaters nor adulterers nor men who have sex with men nor thieves nor the greedy nor drunkards nor slanderers nor swindlers will inherit the kingdom of God.*

I think that makes it pretty clear!

Demons or evil spirits cannot be described in human words, but they are real—they do exist. There are demons in every part of this world. They were at one time angels or some other host of heaven, but they were thrown out with lucifer or satan. Lucifer was one of the most powerful angels at one time and he was beautiful, but he was cast out because of his pride. He wanted to become like God, and almost a third of the heavenly hosts were cast out with him. That does not mean they were all angels because heaven has all kinds of beings in it, not just angels. Demons became so ugly and strong because they have been here on earth for thousands or millions of years, yet they still have the strength they had in heaven, and they have been in hell a long time. Think about living in hell for thousands of years and knowing it will be millions and millions and billions of years and then eternity—you will never get out. That is why the demons are like they are. At one time they may have been beautiful creatures or beings living in heaven, but now being doomed to hell forever has changed them.

Here is a shock for you—over one half of all people going to hell didn't believe in hell before they died. They thought everyone would go to heaven and that hell was what we lived like on earth or what we made of life here on earth. People who believe in gods like statues, rocks, idols—Buddhists, Muslims, Hindus, etc.— are all living a lie, and when they die they are going to be so shocked to find out that there really is a heaven and hell and there really is a God. God is not a rock or a statue, Buddha or Muhammad. He is God, the I AM, the only living God who always has been and always will be, none before and none after Him! You don't have to take my word for this—it's in the Bible. Or you can wait till you go to hell and then you will know what I am telling you is correct— but then it will be too late.

The longer I was staying there in hell, people were grabbing ahold of me, biting me, and screaming at me. Different demons were now attaching themselves to me as well. I could feel them pulling from different directions while the one main spirit continued to hold on to my left wrist. He continually yelled at me, making fun of me and telling me that I was a loser, just like I was always told I would be. I knew now that I was lost for sure, there was no return. I was lost, and to think I had all those chances to turn things around and change my life, but my own self-satisfaction was too important to me. I thought what a fool I had been; I was truly trapped and now would have to pay the price for all eternity.

CHAPTER 6

ARRIVING IN HEAVEN

LL OF A SUDDEN, I HEARD A VOICE LIKE a mighty roar of thunder that said, "It is not his time yet. His mother has been praying for him since he was a little boy. You must release him now; I made a promise!" The evil spirit that had hold of me released me immediately, and I seemed to just fly through space upward and out of hell in seconds. Suddenly there was bright light everywhere; everything glowed. I felt like I had never felt before, wonderful feelings all through my being! Not only did I now have hope, I knew I was in the presence of a heavenly being! I was just outside of this beautiful place, just outside a gate. The gate looked like it was made of pearls and it radiated in beauty, but the light that came from it and from the city inside the gate was unbelievable! It was a light that is not only seen but that penetrates every aspect of your being. The feeling that came over me was so euphoric that nothing in life was sad anymore. I could only feel joy and happiness, no sorrow of any kind. At this time there was nothing holding on to me like in hell, and I had freedom to move around, so I started to go into the gate. As I moved closer, an angel appeared to me and told me I could not stay in heaven. I also now know that my mother's prayers weren't the main reason I didn't stay in hell. I didn't stay in hell because it wasn't my time to die. Hell was a glimpse of what would have been my fate if I didn't change. And now, since I had not changed and given my life to the Lord yet, I had been taken to heaven only to observe, and then tell people on earth about what I saw. I could see everything inside the gates, and I could feel everything everyone else felt, but I wasn't allowed to stay or run around and do things I would have liked.

The angel that stopped me at the gate was a massive being, much like a human but larger than life. He had hair down to his shoulders and was wearing some type of white gown that seemed to glow. His hair was sort of very light brown to a dark blonde and by earthly standards of measurement I would say he was about seven feet tall. When he spoke to me, he had the gentlest voice, yet every word had such power with it. It was clear to me at that point how powerful words are, and I instantly thought about the power of God's words when He speaks. It became easy for me to understand how the whole universe was made just by His spoken word.

When we die there is an odd thing that happens. You instantly know things—everything you ever needed to know, you now know. It would be kind of like being given an entire encyclopedia and knowing everything in it in less than a second. No one has to tell you anything or describe anything to you; you just know it through your whole being. Our spirit, as I have learned, doesn't have a brain to mess things up. We get the same thinking capacity as heavenly beings have without our brains trying to analyze everything first; you just know it and accept it.

This beautiful angel began to tell me some things about my life and what I need to do when I get back on earth. When he spoke to me, I understood everything and knew exactly what I was supposed to do when I was sent back, yet I wanted to stay. Many things he told to me or showed me I cannot discuss with you yet as I was told to keep them to myself until a time when I will be told it's okay to share it. However, there are some things I can share with you at this time.

First, I saw my father in a hospital room. The room was painted a pale yellow and my dad's bed was to the right of the room. There was an older woman there whom I did not recognize as well as a few other people. My dad was lying in the bed with his eyes closed when he suddenly sat straight up, pointing at me, and said, "I did it to you! I did it to you!" This scared me and I asked why I had to see this, and the angel spoke to me about generational curses and sin on earth and told me when I get back to earth I will need to break that curse and sin. The generational curse is a link to your past before you were born; it goes to the third or fourth generation and sometimes even further, depending on what it is and when it began.

I was given several gifts in heaven. One gift is to be able to see inside a person, deep into their soul or spirit. This is not something that I turn on or off, nor can I select the person I can see into; that is up to God. This is not just reserved for church—it happens all the time at work, play, shopping, or anywhere I go. I know it sounds kind of freaky, but it was given to me for a reason. When God gives you a gift, whether it may be singing, teaching, preaching, a kind spirit, a pleasant voice—no matter what it is, use it! God gives us all different gifts, and I know it hurts Him when He sees people who won't use what He gave them or use it for the wrong purpose, but His gifts are irrevocable. What I see is the person's spirit, especially during times of worship. There are many things I see that I never say to a person unless the Holy Spirit gives me the go-ahead; that's just how it works.

I was also shown things about the future. I saw what seemed like millions of people connected to each other with these things at desks and on their laps, and they were typing on them. Remember now, this was in back the '70s and personal computers and laptops did not exist back then. I saw people all over the world connected by something like a big net linking them to each other. People could connect with other people and talk to them through these devices and see the other person on their little TVs.

In 1978, many of these things seemed very strange to me. People were walking around talking to each other on phones that had no wires attached, and later with these little things stuck in the ear, and then later in time people were talking into thin air; nothing I could see was attached to them. Then it was shown to me that they had this little device that had been implanted inside their ear with a little machine and all they had to do was tap on the back or bottom of their ear and say a person's name and they could talk to that person. There was another device that looked like a small, flat TV that was very thin that people walked around with, talking to it and typing on it. There were many people who were all alone, walking and looking at these little phones or flat TVs, typing on them, talking into them. So many people had forgotten how to really communicate, and this was all part of the devil's plan to get control of people because if they forgot how to communicate verbally then they would forget how to pray as well. Connect and keep them in touch with machines instead of people. I also saw buildings in space circling the earth as well as other things I will discuss as I am given permission to do so.

During this time, it was also revealed to me that our nation would go through some very difficult problems, almost to the point of no return, but Christians all across the country started praying and taking action to turn it around. Some were persecuted for their stance, yet it did not stop the Christians from moving forward.

As the angel spoke to me and showed me certain things, I saw so much that I really had no concept of once I returned to my body. But I do know that it all made sense to me at the time. When the angel spoke of things, my awareness was clear and it was easy to understand. I remember that, but once I came back into my body, my mind couldn't grasp it. Even the things in hell made sense while I was there, but when I returned to my body I had confusion about some things because I couldn't understand all of them with my brain; it just doesn't function as well as our spiritual being or mind does. It took a lot of prayer and the Holy Spirit to help make things clear.

It is impossible to express how I felt while being in heaven. It was a euphoric feeling all the time, and speaking of time, there never seemed to be time. Now I understand where it says in the Bible "a thousand years are like a day." Time really has no meaning in heaven; time is something that was made for man here on earth so he could keep records of things he did and when. God's timing is perfect and no calendar or clock can tell you when that is going to be. Yes, we have precise times and dates when the Lord says to do certain things or to show up at particular places at specified times, but that is just for us here on earth; time means nothing in heaven, there isn't day or night, it just always is.

Now I want to tell you what I saw in heaven. Most of my time was spent with this angel, but I did have time to look around some. What I noticed was that the light in heaven was everywhere—there were no shadows, no dark spots in heaven. I saw many huge homes, not like homes here in the United States, but huge structures made with pure white stone of some kind. The streets may have been gold, but the shiniest pure gold you have ever seen. There was a river flowing through heaven, and the water was so clean and pure that it almost looked like nothing was in the river at first. The sound of the water was like little children laughing and singing. Every noise I heard in heaven made me smile and filled me with joy!

There were trees in heaven—two very big, beautiful trees right next to the river running through heaven. On one tree there was one kind of fruit and on the other tree there was a different kind of fruit. Many stopped and looked up at the trees, but I did not see anyone picking fruit off of either tree. The leaves on the trees were like huge magnolia leaves, but much bigger. They were about three or more feet long, and the branches stretched out for what seemed to be miles.

Now let me explain something here. Because there is no real concept of time, space, or distance in heaven and hell, I am just trying to take what I saw and put it in perspective so you can understand. When you die, all these things will become clear because your mind will not be there to interfere with what your spirit knows and comprehends. Our mind is only capable of understanding what we feed it, much like a computer, except that unlike a computer we can try to reason with things and make some changes, but still only with what we already know. In our spirit, we have the ability to understand things that are way beyond our finite minds. We can grasp things of the universe that as humans we have not yet seen nor can we see or understand until we die and are in the spirit. Many things I saw I cannot convey in words. I can't even begin to tell you what they were or even how to describe them. Our minds are limited, but our spirits are not!

I'm sure most of you have heard of the book of Revelation in the Bible. What John saw cannot be described completely in words, though he tries so hard to explain things. I am sure everything he wrote was 100 percent accurate, but if it was someone from today writing of those same visions, maybe it would be described differently because of things that have been invented since then. And what Ezekiel saw—perhaps that would be described differently today. When I saw what I now recognize as computers, tablets, and laptops, I thought there were little flat TVs with some kind of flat typewriters connected to them or tablets with an electronic typewriter inside it, and laptops were the strangest looking things to me as well as tablets. What I found so odd about laptops and tablets was that people had these things with them all over the place and no electricity was hooked up to many of them. People had them with them outside, by a lake, out on a boat, in the woods, all over. As I stated earlier on, I had no idea what a computer was because they didn't have home computers or laptops back then.

CHAPTER 7

ANGELS, MUSIC, AND MORE

IN HEAVEN I LEARNED THAT THERE ARE many different types of angels. One type of angel is much like you and me; they are about the same size as our spirits and they look like us. These angels are given unique assignments to specific people and they can be assigned more than one person at a time. I call them Helper angels. They are there to help you through different things in your life on earth. They can transform into looking just like you, if need be.

There are also Guardian angels. They are usually assigned to one person at a time and they are there to physically guard you from harm. You have heard people tell stories about how they were heading into an accident that couldn't be avoided and the next thing they knew they were outside of the accident unharmed. That is because of these Guardian angels. Sometimes, though, these angels cannot perform their assignment because the person they are watching over has done something to where the angel can't do their job anymore. I will try to explain more on this later.

There are also angels with feathers, or Winged angels. They are usually sent with a particular message to bring to a person or group of people. For example, Winged angels were the ones who announced Jesus' birth, and they are the ones mentioned many times in the Bible who give someone a message from God. I'm sure most of you have heard about angels that show up at places in different churches around the world; that is usually this type of angel. There are also other very important angels that don't have wings that can also bring messages to people; it's just that most messengers are Winged angels.

There are angels whose only assignment is to take answers to prayers back to you. When you pray for something, these angels will be the ones to give you the answers directly from heaven. Some of these angels have been seen, but mostly they are unseen as they carry the message or answer to your prayer. They are very common, and are ascending and descending all the time, 24 hours around the clock. These angels can't make you accept the answers they bring back; that is determined by your will and choice.

Archangels are the biggest and most powerful angels. They usually have one assignment at a time and that assignment usually changes life as we know it here on earth. When you come into the presence of an Archangel you can feel its power; you know they represent God firsthand. The power they possess can actually change the course of time and events here on earth. If you saw an Archangel here on earth it would scare you to death. But in heaven, your spirit understands this power and that its power comes from God, not to be feared in heaven. There were very few Archangels that I saw; only three of them were visible to me.

I also saw angels whose only purpose is to worship God. They just sing praises to God and their voices are, well, angelic. There is no other way to explain it; their voices combined together would make anyone hearing it feel euphoric. I saw many more angels there. I didn't know their specific purposes. I only understood the few I just described. There are just so many things that can be understood in the spirit that can never be put into words through the processes of one's mind because the human brain simply can't comprehend it.

The music in heaven is not like what we heard in churches back while I was growing up, or even the new contemporary music back in the '70s; it was more like chants and praises! I can tell you that songs like "Holy" that Jesus

Culture sings and some music from Elevation and other groups now is more like what you hear in heaven, but without the heavy electric guitar. It is total worship. The kind of music is all praise music, not like "The Old Rugged Cross" or hymns; everything is happy and praise-style sounds. Think about it—you are in heaven, God and Jesus are there, and you have everything you could ever want or need, so why not praise! Since I have been back on earth, nothing moves me more than music now, because I know the source of praise and I am constantly seeking that beautiful sound I heard while I was in heaven.

Here on earth we get tired of things in a short time, but in heaven the people there are so full of the Spirit of God—because they are completely spirit and have no fleshly mind to tire them out or bring them down—that it's 24/7 praise and worship! I tried a lot of different drugs back in the '70s, and there wasn't anything that could give you even one one-millionth of a percent of a high like you get in heaven. Without your flesh to hold you back or to bring thoughts of sinful things into your mind, there is nothing but praise and worship left in you. Your spirit wells up and you just start singing and praising God!

Some music made me want to jump up and shout, while other times it was simply soothing and melodious to the spirit. I heard music that was so soft and gentle that it would just float through my spirit as if it were a gentle breeze caressing me the whole time. No one in heaven sings off-key; everyone has perfect pitch. Our voices go up as one when we sing there. Though we all sing different parts—bass, tenor, alto, and soprano—it all blends together as one voice. And something I was so excited about is that we do actually get to sing with the angels!

The feeling you have when you are in heaven is something that you don't ever want to go away; you never want to leave heaven. I am bringing this up again because I feel it's important to know that feelings are part of our spirit, not just our physical bodies. How many times have you heard people say, "You can't just go on feelings"? In heaven, that is not true—you can go just on feelings because your spirit doesn't have a fleshly mind like it does on earth. Your spirit hears, thinks, tastes, feels, and smells throughout your whole being, so feelings are hard to ignore once you have experienced dying and being in the spirit. Feelings in heaven are the norm. Here on earth they tell you not to trust your feelings because your flesh has sin in it.

You have to understand, what we have on earth that we can see or figure out with our minds are only things of the flesh, but the spiritual world is more alive, even here, than you can see. Spirits in this world are not all from God; there are many false spirits and many very evil spirits. Most of the time you can tell when someone has the Spirit of God in them and you can tell when someone is evil, but when you die and experience it firsthand, you have a much greater awareness and knowledge of spiritual things when you come back to earth. It's kind of like the difference between someone who has never cooked a day in their life and a professional chef. Now the chef is experienced and he or she knows how to prepare, season, and cook the food, but the person who has never cooked might know what those foods are and they may have tasted them before, but they have no idea how to fix them. What I am getting at is this—once you have experienced something, you have greater knowledge than someone who hasn't. An astronaut can tell you what it is like to experience being in space, but all we can do is imagine it or look at footage on film or video. Until we go there, we really can't experience it. Sure, we can go someplace and have a simulated space experience, but that's not the same thing. I have met a couple other people who have died before and experienced heaven and they understand immediately what I mean when I say that our earthly minds can't understand, comprehend, or conceive what our spirit knows. Therefore, trust the Spirit of God in you and don't worry about it. God knows what He is doing!

CHAPTER 8

WHAT HEAVEN WAS LIKE

THIS IS GOING TO BE DIFFICULT, BECAUSE nothing we have on earth compares. In heaven there is no darkness and no shadows of any kind. Imagine light being everywhere. You walk under a tree and it is just as light as standing out in direct sunlight. You look up through the leaves of the tree and there are no shadows between the leaves—the light engulfs everything. Because of this, colors look different in heaven, more vibrant and pure. Nothing on earth can compare to the light or colors in heaven, and our earthly minds cannot explain or comprehend what it looks like.

Some people say the streets are gold, but the reality is it's difficult to say what they are made of because everything there is so shiny and bright. The buildings there appeared to be made of some kind of white marble. Inside the houses or mansions, the light is just as bright as it is outside. As I walked around in heaven I was looking everywhere, including down at my feet. The streets I walked on just glowed like a high-gloss gold, but it didn't feel like gold. It was actually soft. I won't even begin to tell you what the grass or flowers looked like. My brain cannot find the words to describe them, but I can tell you that walking on the grass barefoot was a rush. The grass was so soft—like walking on a cloud!

You can float in heaven. All you do is pick your feet up and think about floating and you do—it's effortless. You could soar as high as any eagle or airplane here on earth, but in heaven it's not a big deal—it's like walking. Every movement you make is effortless. You never get tired and you can always be on the move. Oh, how I wish that were true on earth!

When you look toward what seems to be the center of heaven, you see this light that surpasses anything you have ever seen. The light has warmth, like the feeling of honey flowing all over you, without the stickiness. You can see forever and hear things that you could never hear on earth. Can you imagine a place where no fear exists? No sickness, no sorrow, no sadness, not any form of depression of any kind—everyone was happy all the time!

In heaven you instantly know things, like who someone is, without anyone saying a thing to you. I saw some of the people from the Bible moving around. I know I saw Elisha, John the Baptist, Matthew, and Luke. I did not speak to any of them; I just saw them going about heaven. You see, I wasn't supposed to be there yet, or at least I wasn't allowed to stay there. The angel stayed with me wherever I went, and I didn't go too far from the gate. I saw many other people too, but we did not talk. It was so great not to have to talk to someone and ask them their name—I just knew it, even if they walked by me.

One name sticks out and I don't know why. She was not anyone from the Bible days or anyone I knew about before. Her name was Esther Remington. I hope someone reading this will know something about her or why it was important to remember her name. She died when she was old, but she looked so young now. She was a very loving woman on earth. I believe Esther was from California and had died a few years before I arrived in heaven, maybe late 1960s or early 1970s.

Once you have actually been to heaven, you have a different outlook on life than anyone else. You see things differently and understand things others cannot. Your passion for life and people is magnified when you come back, and you have an understanding and a compassion you never had before. You know how important it is to talk to people and win souls for the Lord, because after you die it is too late.

I was given several gifts in heaven, but the most awesome gift any of us can ever have and the only gift you can take with you to heaven is—Love!

CHAPTER 9

DEEPER EXPERIENCES IN HEAVEN

THERE WAS SOMETHING ELSE I NOTICED IN heaven. Everyone there seemed to know each other, and when someone new came to heaven there would often be people they had known on earth who greeted them when they arrived. This occurred most of the time, but some people were met by angels and other heavenly hosts. It was exciting to see people getting greeted when they got to heaven!

Watching children being met by their parents or children who had died young meeting their mother or father who died after them—this included children who had been aborted or miscarriage—that was really exciting to see! When a husband would meet his wife or wife meet her husband, what joy! No tears, just the joy that floods all of heaven. To answer the question most ask at reading this, "Does that mean you're married in heaven?" The answer is no. But you do recognize the one you were married to and are happy to see them just like anyone else in your family.

There are beings in heaven other than God, Jesus, the Holy Spirit, us, and the angels. There are other heavenly beings that I find too difficult to describe, and others that I will attempt to give my best description. There are beings that walk around heaven just praising the Lord. They look like nothing we have on earth to compare them with, but they are beautiful and sing with power and authority. They go around heaven making sure that praises of God are being lifted up in every section of heaven. They are human-like with big, beautiful eyes, and they have small, chubby legs and arms—kind of like a chubby little baby with a rather big mouth. They just seem to float around in heaven as they sing.

There was one being that I could not get close enough to, which makes it difficult for me to describe it very well to you, but it had many eyes on it—in fact, thousands of eyes or more all over its body and wings. I could see the eyes going back and forth as if looking for something or someone, and although at the time I understood clearly the purpose, now I am unsure what it was. This being was much further in toward the middle of heaven.

Closer toward what I would call the center of heaven was this very bright light, brighter than our sun, but it did not hurt me to look at it; it was kind of like looking at lightning, so pure and white. The feeling I got when I gazed at that light was so pure and overwhelming with nothing but love—a love like I had never before experienced. I felt like I was being drawn to it, like it just pulled at everything inside me to go to it, but I was not allowed to go that far because I had not done what I needed to do on earth to be allowed up there to stay. I wish I could somehow convey the feeling that came over me; it was so powerful and soothing at the same time. I knew that I was in the presence of the Holy of Holies in heaven.

I can remember the sounds, smells, and feelings of heaven as I walked around there; it's something I will never forget as long as I live. I recall the laughter, singing, praises, and beautifulness of everything and everybody.

If you are reading this and you are not a Christian, I strongly suggest you make a change in your life here on earth, because this life goes by in just a snap of the fingers and your afterlife is forever. I am not talking about just as long as a hundred years or so, but for all eternity—forever and ever. That's longer than it would take you to walk around the world a million times; in fact, that would be less than a second in heaven. Get my point? This is real. Heaven and hell are the final destinations and my question is—which one do you want to be in forever? I'm not trying to get religious on you; I'm trying to save your life. Think about it while you finish reading this book.

There were some other things I was shown in heaven about the future of our earth. There were people on earth who were there strictly to corrupt the world, the leaders, and the common people. These people were possessed of a spirit that leads people into false hopes and delusions. Many people on earth believed these leaders as they convinced the people of earth that everything would be good for them if they just trusted them.

As we know today, in the United States, this is very much like the leaders of the Democrat party. There is a great socialist, Marxist group that is trying to bring in communism to the United States, disguised as socialists or "The Party" that wants to give away everything for free. This far left party is trying to take over the Democrat party and will pull in some members of the Republican party by lying to them and trying to make deals with them. I saw this from heaven and it is happening now and will go on for some time.

Homosexuality was coming to a peak in the future where it seemed the majority of people were accepting it and the ones who didn't were actually being persecuted and prosecuted in many parts of the world. The LGBTQ and other groups have infiltrated all segments of Hollywood, our education system, and many churches. It is a lie from the pit of hell! LGBTQ is an agenda to eventually bring in pedophilia and other sex agendas as "being normal." This angered God!

The other spirit that was entering into people caused them to lust after children, and parents gave their children away to others who said they loved their children. Some parents even sold their children to these evil and vile people. Not only were men seeking these children, but women, too. Some wanted to perform homosexual acts on these children and others heterosexual sexual acts on them. This was being accepted in many parts of the world, and it greatly angered God, too!

What you must understand is I saw these things back in 1978, long before any of this was known on earth. What I saw people doing in the future to children made me so sick that I almost can't even write about it. They are actually raising children up for these sick and disgusting practices. Women are having children to be raised as sex slaves and they are "programmed" or brainwashed into the world from day one. They are taught not to believe anyone except their handler. Some children are being raised just to be sacrificed.

There was another spirit of lust that was prevalent in the world and that was a lust for power and control. This lust came out of the Middle East and was spreading around the world at an alarming rate. It was disguised as a form of religion and relied heavily on recruiting young people believing in the lies they were told of wonderful places and experiences they would have if they just obeyed. It was the ultimate mind control of our youth. An army was being raised to take over the world one place at a time, but wearing down all the earth as much as possible. Many of these were little children. From the time of their birth, they were told that Christians were the enemy. Some of these children attended schools that taught them not to love anyone who was not of their faith, but to hate them. However, this spirit of lust for control and power will never be successful because the Spirit of God will not allow it, and the people of this earth will eventually revolt.

I saw Israel standing alone; many nations had separated themselves from Israel, yet Israel had done nothing wrong to deserve it. Even the United States was taking action that harmed Israel. I saw many European nations take a stand against Israel as well. All these European nations and the United States finally turned things around, but only after some damage was already done. These nations changed their minds after they realized they had been lied to and used. I saw lies, lies, and more lies coming out of the Middle East. Israel was the only nation telling the truth!

You will see that some of the Middle East countries will back off of Israel, but some will not. There will be some real peace in parts of the Middle East, that seemed impossible, but it will come. First by one nation, then a next and a next and so on. Be very cautious of Iran and Syria as in the future Russia and China will try to use them.

Many of the things I saw then, in my visit to heaven, have now come to pass and have angered God. The people of the earth need a wakeup call, and that is coming soon. There will be great storms, earthquakes, and many more natural disasters that will occur not just in the United States but in the entire world. Remember, these things were revealed to me back in 1978 before the big 9.0 earthquake struck Japan, and the tsunamis, and the worst typhoon in recorded history that hit the Philippine Islands. I can tell you that these events are just the beginning, but those who are solid in the Lord and really do put Him first will be warned. The angel showed me that there are a few people on earth right now that know about these things and that they are the intercessors praying for our country. These are not necessarily the big evangelists or TV preachers, but regular individuals who are the intercessors on their face before the Lord daily. Now, there are going to be some major preachers who are going to finally stand up against this filth and immorality, but that time is still to come. I was not to know the exact times when these things would happen, but I am certainly aware that it has started.

Another thing that was shown to me was the spirit of deception within the church, accompanied by the spirit of self-righteousness. There were people of all religions belonging to churches who were going around trying to divide up the church in order to satisfy their own righteousness. They would go to other individuals in the church and spread lies and rumors about certain ministers in the church, attacking the pastors and worship leaders. These rumors would spread like wildfire. Even those who knew better would start believing because the spirit of deception was so strong, and the people of the church were not prayed up enough to know the difference. Satan is well aware that if he can divide the church, he can conquer it and steal people away. However, this too will come to a stop by the power of the Holy Spirit. The people trying to do this will be exposed and they will be accountable for the ones they led astray unless they repent.

Something else the angel talked to me about was hidden intentional sin. These are sins that people who claim to be Christians do frequently on a regular basis. Let me explain— if you are a Christian, you know right from wrong from the Holy Spirit indwelling within you. But if you think that right and wrong are only what other people see in you, you are deceiving yourself. What has been happening is that many people are claiming one thing and behind closed doors are doing another. If you are looking at porn, treating your family badly, cheating on your spouse, are into violent or graphic gaming, using illegal drugs or abusing prescription drugs, or drinking alcoholic beverages daily, and you are hiding these things, then that is your hidden intentional sin. These are not the only ones; there are many more, like aggravating your children, lusting after your fellow coworker, cussing, anything that you would not do in front of Jesus if He were standing next to you. Doing these things over and over again when you know it is wrong—that is intentional sinning.

Hidden intentional sinning has become one of the worst epidemics in the Christian community; it surpasses anything close to it by a mile. The angel said that this displeases God greatly and He wants it made known. He said that if people do not repent, then He will expose them, from the top evangelist on down to the quietest person at church. I want to further elaborate that I am not talking about sin that is unintentional; I am talking about sin that you know is wrong, yet you intentionally choose to repeat the behavior. You are not fooling anyone but yourself. Believe it or not, many times people know that you are doing it, but they don't say anything because they don't want to embarrass you. Don't you think you are going to hate it when it is exposed to everyone and they all find out what you are doing? I mean, what if you are beating your spouse, looking at porn or lusting after someone while you are married—do you really want that exposed? Do you?

For me, it's a little different; I have been charged with warning you because I have been there, and you don't want to go to hell! I am being sent with this warning—either you repent and change your ways, or it will be exposed. The time for you to take heed to what I am saying is now; you have been warned by reading this book.

Let me ask you a question—if you saw a three-year-old child walking along the side of the road and they turn to walk directly into oncoming traffic going 75 miles per hour, what would you do? Would you just keep driving away looking in the other direction and hope someone else will stop and help them, or think maybe they will magically make it through to the other side? I would be willing to bet most of you would you come to a screeching halt, jump out of your car, and rescue them. That is what I am doing by warning you about this. This is the most stoppable sin there is, because you already know it's wrong and you know the right way to go, so please stop before it's too late! You have no idea how many people I saw in hell who didn't belong there—or at least, they didn't think they did. Hidden intentional sin has been rampant for many years now and getting worse every day, especially with all the new technology continually coming out. In the near future this technology will even produce human-like forms that will be part of the worst lust the word has ever seen.

CHAPTER 10

BACK TO EARTH

So many things we don't know here on earth will all be revealed to us when we get to heaven. I can tell you there is no sorrow, no pain, and no regret in heaven. I wish I could explain everything as I saw it and felt it, but it is beyond what the human mind can comprehend. When you get to heaven you will not be worrying about your children or other loved ones here on earth because you will be in the presence of God, and that is something that just can't be explained.

I do want to tell you more about why I was spared from hell, and it has nothing to do with me or my cries for help while in hell. The real reason I didn't stay in hell was because it wasn't my time to die. As I said before, my experience in hell was a glimpse of where I would have ended up if I didn't change and give my life to Jesus. The angel that spoke to me in heaven also told me that God was honoring my mother's prayers because she had been so faithful to God in her life and had said over 20,000 prayers for me, and God made her a promise about her children. She prayed for me two to three times daily. Can you imagine being prayed for 20,000 times? My mother is a godly woman and brought all of her children up in the ways of the Lord and in church. The paths we took may not have been right, but she knew that if she raised us in the ways of the Lord we would all return someday if we drifted away. Mom, you were right about that one!

This angel explained to me that everyone who goes to hell cries out for God but that it is too late for them. My escape from hell was one in a million, and it wasn't because of anything I did on earth or how I lived. It's because it wasn't my time to die, and because of my mother's prayers. Parents, never stop praying for your children. Even when it looks impossible, keep praying for them and never give up.

When the angel was finished telling me things, it allowed me to stand just inside the gate and view what heaven was like for some time. Oh, I did not want to leave, I didn't want to go back to earth; this was so beautiful and wonderful. The music that you hear literally goes though you—you feel the music and the singing; it pierces every part of your being and it is so beautiful and uplifting! I thought, "Please God, I don't want to go back to earth," but I could not stay there because I had to change my life in order to get back to heaven and I had a job to do—write this book.

The final thing the angel told me was, "You must wait to tell about your experience until you are told to do so." I understood that this was a warning and I also knew that my life was not where it was supposed to be and that I needed to turn things around.

Back to earth I went, and in a blink of an eye I was entering my bedroom. There in the room were two paramedics who had just arrived. One paramedic was feeling my neck for a pulse, and he shook his head looking back over his right shoulder to the other paramedic standing behind him. The man behind him was getting something out of a medical bag while the one who checked my pulse was getting ready to turn me onto my back, as I was lying on my left side facing toward a wall. Just then my spirit moved into my body and started to wake it up. It shook my body violently, vibrating like I had just been hit with electricity, and it actually scared the paramedics. All of a sudden, I was able to breathe, and I opened my eyes and stared straight at this surprised paramedic. I will never forget the look on his face as he asked, "Are you alright?" in a startled voice. I replied that I was, though I was in some kind of shock because I was back in my body here on earth. It was difficult for me to speak or move much at first.

They insisted on checking me thoroughly, and after about twenty minutes or so they could not find anything wrong with me and they left. First, though, they tried to get me to go with them to the hospital, but I refused to go. I was aware that something significant had occurred and I was trying my best to sort it all out but wasn't afraid to stay at home; I knew nothing else would happen to me. By the way, I did say a quick, short prayer, "Lord, forgive me of my sins, I accept Jesus as my Lord and Savior. Amen!"

I could not sleep the rest of that night; I didn't want to smoke any more pot or do anything except sit there and wonder about what just happened to me. The paramedics had told me that my girlfriend called around 11:45 p.m. and they got there in about five minutes. My body was cold to the touch and blue. I had no pulse and wasn't breathing; I was dead. They also told me that they had never seen anyone do what I did when I came back to life, vibrating like I did—it startled them. I was trying to wake my body up, shake it, whatever I had to do because it was so stiff, and I couldn't breathe.

I sat up all night in a little avocado-green rocking chair crying my eyes out to God. It was the most emotional time I have had in my life. I cried because I was so sorry for what I had done wrong and so glad that God gave me a second chance, a real second chance!

The next morning about 6:00, I got up and went to the hospital to see the doctor who had been treating me for the blood clot. I arrived there around 6:30 a.m., no traffic at all at that time in the morning in Grand Rapids, Michigan. The doctor had an office that he used for consultations at the hospital, and I sat on the floor waiting till he came in so I could talk to him. A little after 7:00 the doctor arrived, and I asked him if I could please talk to him before he started his rounds. He agreed, and we went into his office as I started to tell him what happened to me.

You have to understand I was scared to death, thinking I was going nuts or something. I talked for what seemed like over an hour as the doctor listened to me with such interest. Then I asked him, "Am I nuts, or did this really happen to me?" I did not tell the doctor details, just general information like being in hell and seeing horrible things and then being in heaven and seeing angels, etc.

I can remember the doctor clearly telling me, "What happened to you, I believe, was real. I am not saying that you just think it is real; I am saying it really happened." He went on to tell me that he'd had a couple patients who had died and come back to life and they told him things similar to what I told him, except they had not gone to hell. I was the first to tell him about hell. He also explained that the clot was so big that he had worried when the blood was thinned out that some of the clot would move into my heart or my lungs. That was the reason they had kept me at the hospital for two weeks.

CHAPTER 11

NOW WHAT
DO I DO?

NOW WHAT DO I DO?" I WONDERED. I HAD died, gone to hell, and then to heaven. I thought, "Who is ever going to believe this?" I was very confused, but I kept remembering what the angel had told me just before coming back to earth: "You must wait to tell about your experience until you are told to do so." I had no idea when that was going to be. I was hoping that by 1980 I would be ready, but I was far from it then. It wasn't until 1994 that I turned my life completely around to the Lord. Now don't get me wrong—I had stopped drinking and doing drugs, and I had quit sleeping around with so many women and a lot of other sinful things before 1994, but it wasn't until August of 1994 when I finally made a 100-percent commitment to God.

In July of 1994 I moved my family from Nashville, Tennessee to Albuquerque, New Mexico. I was married and had a son named Christopher who had been born in 1985. I taught Christopher how to pray, to ask the blessing over the food, and I taught him about Jesus. But I hadn't taken him to church. I remember that in August of 1994, a new neighbor named Dana came over and introduced herself to us and invited us to attend her church. I knew it was time to start doing that—going to church. Christopher was eight at the time, about to turn nine in December. He needed to know more about the Lord, and I knew it was the right thing to do, especially because he needed to be around kids his age so they could learn things about the Lord together.

That August, Dana and her husband, Nick, invited us over to dinner and to play *Bible Pictionary*. Well, I had been raised in church and had actually been in heaven, so I thought I would do well at this game. As it turned out, it was the *Bible Pictionary* game for children that we played, and I did horrible. Talk about being shocked—everyone else knew the answers and I didn't remember them until after they were answered by someone else. I felt like a fool. That night I decided I was never going to be that bad at this game again, so I decided to start reading the Bible.

The very next morning I got up early, opened my Bible, and started reading from Genesis chapter one, verse one. I had decided that I was going to read it from cover to cover. I was told that if I just read three chapters of the Bible each day I would be able to read the whole Bible in one year. I thought, "Hey, I can do that." So I read all three chapters that morning and every morning for a whole year—well, almost. There were times, like when I got to Psalm 119, that I only read that one chapter, but other days I read four or five to make up for it.

A year was over, and I can still remember when I finished reading that last verse in Revelation 22, verse 21, "The grace of the Lord Jesus be with God's people. Amen." Whoopee! I had just finished reading the whole Bible! I can remember thinking to myself, "Wow, Ivan, how many other people have actually read every word in the Bible from cover to cover?"

I was so proud of this accomplishment! Then it was like a voice I could hear say, "Now what?"

I thought, "Now what? I read the whole Bible. That's what's *now what*."

Then I heard that voice again, "So what all do you remember?"

I answered, "Well, I remember about Adam and Eve, and Noah, and Moses, and Job, and about Jesus, and other things."

And the voice said, "What can you quote?"

Well, that didn't go over well with me because the only scripture I could quote was John 3:16, "For God so loved the world that he gave his one and only Son, that whoever believes in him shall not perish but have eternal life."

So I knew I needed more work on that part, and then I heard the voice again. "Read it again." Read it again? But I just finished it! "Read it again," the voice said one more time. Okay, I got the message and started all over again to read it and have been doing that just about every year since 1994.

Here's something I learned about reading the Bible—there is something new in it every day no matter how many times you read it. My Bible is so worn down, marked up, and falling apart, but it is still my Bible and I discover new meaning in it every single day! I knew one day that I would like to pass this old marked-up, torn-up Bible to my son, Christopher, and that day was Christmas of 2014.

It is clear to me now that I had to mature— not just as a person but spiritually as well. I used to wonder why the Lord was not allowing me to write this book about what I went through, but it has now become very clear to me that I needed to first be rooted in the Word and in my prayer life. I have made a lot of mistakes since 1978 and have often wondered why I made all those mistakes when I knew better. I guess it just goes to show that our human nature needs to constantly be kept in check, and I was not doing that very well for a while.

Over the last ten years I have spent many days and nights on my face before the Lord, and I have been studying the Word of God more. My walk with the Lord is so strong now, especially after the Lord removed some things out of my life to clear the way for me to write this book.

I mention this because many churches today are so concerned about the show they put on and not as concerned about what the people attending need. If all you get is a twenty-minute sermon and three to five songs every week, how is that really helping your people? We need to seek the face of God.

Right now, we need real prayer time with God, and I am not talking about us asking God for things, but time to just pray in the Spirit. The Spirit knows, much more than our minds, what we need. Corporate prayer is great and it is needed, but we also need much more time on our faces before the Lord.

Back when I was a kid, we used to have real prayer services where we really sought after the Lord. Sometimes we would start out praying at 7:00 in the evening and not finish until midnight. Every New Year's Eve we would gather at church around 9:00 p.m. for some songs and a few words from our pastor, and then we would get on our knees and pray in the New Year and not leave until 1:00 or 2:00 in the morning. Today, most churches that have a New Year's Eve service just have a quick service and off you go; they start to flicker the lights fifteen minutes after midnight to let you know it's time to leave. I am not saying we need to be like we used to be, but we do need to get serious about the Lord.

There are new moves of the Spirit of the Lord and the old ways do not fit in the new ways, like the new wine does not fit into the old wineskins. We must adapt, but we should never lose sight of worship and spending time in prayer. Think about this—how many times in the New Testament do you read about Jesus praying? I mean, after all, He is the Son of God; did He really need to pray? Well, if Jesus needed it, then so do we! We need it a lot more than Jesus did and we seem to think that all we need to do is say a little prayer every night and ask the blessing before or after each meal and we are good to go, but I am telling you that is not enough. Jesus is coming back for a church that is ready for Him, not a group of people who are lukewarm.

What I am getting at is this—I have been to hell and heaven and I know I need a lot more of God in my life. I cannot disappoint Him anymore. Many of you reading this book know that you need to turn up the fire in your life too. Quit playing church or playing games. Search your heart and make a decision to turn up the heat in your own life. It doesn't matter what church you go to, but it does matter what you are being taught and how much time you put into the Lord. The church is not going to save you or get you to heaven; that is up to you *only!*

The old style of pastors doing everything at the church is changing and it needs to change. We are the church, not that building you walk into every Sunday. We need to all be more active in what we do. It is not up to the pastor of the church to minister to everyone; that is our job as Christians, but you can't do it if you aren't prayed up and read up.

There is a new move of the Holy Spirit that is beginning to spread throughout the world, and if you just go to church on Sunday and maybe Wednesday night services and you aren't exploring more on your own about the move of the Spirit, you are going to miss it. In fact, you will be one of those people who will be sitting on the sidelines judging it. Too many people in the past and in the coming future are willing to criticize the move of the Spirit like they know it all and they know everything that God can do and God hasn't checked with them yet to get their approval. I've got news for you—God doesn't need your approval. He's going to do it anyway! Remember, Jesus said to do these things and greater, so how do you get to greater? By reading His Word and spending time in prayer.

Sometimes when I am talking about the Lord and what He's done for me and sharing things I have to say, I have had people ask me, "Who gave you the authority to say that?"

I love the look on their faces when I tell them, "Jesus!"

They get all bent out of shape and twisted up and then they can't help but say, "So are you telling me Jesus talks directly to you?"

"Why yes, He does, and He talks to you, too. In fact, I think He asked your permission yesterday if it was okay to talk to me." That is my reply, and that usually ends that. They have no idea how to answer me after I say that to them. Some get huffy and walk away and others just stare at me trying to come up with an answer, but they never do.

We all serve the same God, and God is not into religion; He is into having a relationship with you. Adam didn't have any religion, yet he talked with God in the Garden. Moses didn't have a religion, yet he spoke directly to God and God used him to deliver His people out of Egypt. It's not religion that is going to get you to heaven; it is your personal walk with the Lord. Here is something simple to do—ask God to allow the Holy Spirit to be your teacher when you read the Bible. That's what I did, and the Holy Spirit was my teacher. He continually opens my eyes and reveals things to me on a daily basis. We also need to quit laying the blame on everyone else for us not being where we are supposed to be with the Lord. It is not someone else's fault; it is our own. Stop blaming that pastor at the church you used to go to—you know, that one who hurt your feelings because he didn't do something the way you wanted him to do it or he said something that offended you. If you keep hanging on to that lie you will be going straight to hell when you die. I promise you, there are a lot of people in hell who fell for this lie just like you.

Hell is not a figment of your imagination and it's not just for really "bad" people; it is also for those who have turned their back on the Lord. I ought to know; I've been there and done that. Why are you going to let other people affect your walk with the Lord? You can't afford it and you don't have time enough in life, either. I was only 26 years old when I died, and I am one of the very rare lucky ones who got to come back and straighten out my life. Hell is for real! Don't keep playing around, or everyone going to your funeral will say, "I sure hope he made it."

I am not God. I can't tell you whether you are going to hell or not. That is solely up to God. But I can tell you these things I have been shown and told so that you can escape hell. I can't tell you if you are going to heaven or not either, but you can decide that yourself by giving your heart to the Lord, accepting Jesus as your Lord and Savior, and then living the life you are supposed to live. Don't believe the lie that you can live like hell after you give your heart to the Lord and still get to heaven.

I am living proof that that doesn't work, and thank God I am living proof because the other people who have done that and died are still in hell—forever. I still get queasy when I think about it.

In 2013, I found out that during that time in my life back in 1978, when I was not living for the Lord, my grandmother had a vision or dream about me. She told my mother and everyone else back then that she saw me standing on a huge rock and I was preaching and singing to thousands of people. My mother never told me about it because she thought my grandmother was crazy. After all, I was not living for the Lord at that time, and my mother knew I was into drugs. For many years, I did not live near my mother or grandmother nor did I ever get a chance to talk to my grandmother on the phone. In the spring of 2013, while talking to my mother on the phone about being an ordained minister, my mother remembered what my grandmother told her and explained how excited my grandmother was and how she was telling everyone in great detail about my preaching and sing-ing. My grandmother had passed away at 94 in 2003, before I could ask her about it. I wonder what she knew and exactly what day she had that dream or vision.

Here is something else to really think about—I have had ADHD all my life. If you know anything about anyone with ADHD, you know they can't keep track of something for more than a few seconds, but us ADHD adults can actually pay attention for up to two min-utes! Can you believe that God has blessed me enough to allow me to sit down and write this book? I'm great at writing TV commercials— they are all thirty or sixty seconds long—but for me this book is like writing a whole movie! There are days when I have sat for six to eight hours straight just typing away. That is unheard of for people like me, but we can do mighty things when God calls us to do it!

CHAPTER 12

MY FATHER

LET ME EXPLAIN TO YOU MORE ABOUT THE relationship between my father and me. My father was born in Hannibal, Missouri back in 1926 and he was raised on a farm. He had a brother, but he got killed in World War II, and he had a sister too, but she died in her early forties from the same heart disease that eventually took my father. My whole family on my dad's side has something called cardiomyopathy. Each of my blood sisters and my only brother have it, their children have it, and so do all of their grandchildren. My son and I do not have it, nor will we ever get it. This has to do with the generational sin and curses I was told to break by the angel in heaven.

My heart was checked around 1974 and they said I had some abnormalities in it. I was told I had a larger left side to my heart than normal, which is a form of cardiomyopathy. I never had any heart attacks or anything, just some pressure once in a while. I did not have a Doppler echo done to my heart back then, but the doctors told me I had this problem. But since I went to heaven and came back and broke the generational curse, I am free of any hint of it.

I'm sure some of you think this is really an odd thing that God can break not only the generational sin but also physical curses in your family tree that are linked to you. This type of cardiomyopathy is a generational curse; it came from my father's maternal side of the family. My grandmother on my father's side died when I was only about a year old from this disease. It has been passed down from one generation to the next for at least four or five generations that we were able to discover, and now it has spread to three more generations.

If you remember, when I was in heaven I saw my father sit up in his hospital bed and he said, "I did it to you. I did it to you." This was part of what he was talking about; he passed on that physical curse of cardiomyopathy to his children. Because I was made aware of what it was and where it came from, I was able through prayer and fasting to break that curse in Jesus' name, and it no longer has power over me. My heart and my blood no longer have any signs of this incurable disease. I have a recent cardiologist report that says that I *do not* have cardiomyopathy in any way, shape, or form!

My oldest sister, Carolyn, had bad problems with it though. She got a heart transplant in 2002, but she only lived one more year. She did not die of a heart problem, but from a brain tumor. She was only 56. Carolyn started the first cardiomyopathy association in the world over in England. She was very successful in teaching people about this condition, even doctors. She was very educated and extremely smart. You can look up Carolyn Biro and the Cardiomyopathy Association in the United Kingdom on the web at http://www .cardiomyopathy.org/Carolyn-Biro.html.

My sisters, my brother, and I had our blood tested for a genetic study to see if they could find the marker in our blood back in 1990. I did not have it because the curse was broken, but everyone else did. Unfortunately, my older sister, Kathy, suffers from the disease now. Kathy's daughter had open-heart surgery when she was in her late twenties to help her heart pump blood properly. The surgery was successful for her; she is in her forties at the writing of this book. Now that you understand this part, let me talk more about my relationship with my father.

In December of 1981 my father and I finally had a healing moment. My father and I both lived in Lakeland, Florida at the time, and my dad had divorced my mother about two years before and eventually married another woman. I called my father up on the phone in early December and asked him if I could come over to visit. He said, "Sure, come on over. I'm just watching TV." So I went over to his house; this was around 10:30 or so in the morning. I knocked on his door and he yelled, "Come on in, it's unlocked." I went inside and said hi to my dad; he was sitting in his easy chair watching some game show on TV. I walked over to the breakfast bar across the room from the front door and sat on a stool. My father asked me, "What are you doing today?"

I said, "I just wanted to come over and talk with you, Dad."

"What about?" he asked.

I decided it was time I found out what made my dad so angry when I was a child. "Dad?" I said, sounding as if I was going to ask a question.

My father said, "What?"

"Dad, I would like to ask for you to forgive me for whatever it was that I did to you as a kid that got you so upset to have to beat me like you did."

You could hear a pin drop—not one sound and no movement from my dad. I thought for sure he was going to blow up at me, and then I saw something I had never seen before—my father was crying. These were not little tears; they were coming out in buckets. Even the front of his shirt was getting soaked. Then he stood up and turned to me and said, "No, forgive me," as he put his arms out to hug me. Needless to say, I started crying too. My father had never hugged me in his life, nor had he ever apologized about anything, and here he was hugging me and saying he was sorry.

This was the first time in my father's life I had ever seen him actually cry, and those tears were for me. He had only shed one tear when his father died, but other than that one tear he'd never cried in front of me, and now he was crying for how he treated me. Thank You, God!

My father then proceeded to tell me why he mistreated me as a child, and he truly wanted forgiveness because he knew it was wrong. My father repented to me that day, and from that day forward he told me things he had never told anyone before; he wanted to set the record straight. For the next five months my father and I had a close relationship where we saw each other several times a week and chatted on the phone a lot too.

Then April 1, 1982 came around and my father had another heart attack. This was maybe his seventh or eighth one, I can't really remember, but his heart was so bad it didn't matter. My dad was going into the hospital and he called me and asked me to meet him there. I left work and went straight there. I can remember him being excited when he saw me. He said he had something to say to me and wanted to do it in private. Finally, the doctors and nurses left the room and my father told me, "Son, I am going to leave here next Wednesday, one way or another. Either they are going to find a way to fix my heart, or I am just going to leave this earth." That was a shocker for me to hear my father say that, as he had always been such a positive person about his condition. At this point his heart was so enlarged it could hardly beat, and my father had always been a very active man.

During his one-week stay, I visited him several times and he told me more things he had never told anyone before. That Tuesday night I called him on the phone and he said, "Tomorrow's the day, one way or another." He still seemed too full of life to be dying, so I never thought much about what he said. Around 6:45 the next morning, Wednesday, April 7, I got a call from the hospital. They told me that my dad was in a coma and I'd better rush down there. I got to the hospital around 7:30 a.m. or so, and his new wife and her daughter were there, as well as some other lady. I felt like I was in the room with a bunch of strangers, wondering what they were doing in there when my father was dying.

I walked around the bed to his right side and held his hand and let him know I was there. I spoke to him, but there was no response. Then a nurse walked in to moni-tor my dad's vital signs, check his pulse, etc. When she lifted up one of his eyelids, I could see his eyes were rolled back. I went out in the hallway and called a preacher friend of mine, and he came up to the hospital around 9:00 that morning. While I was waiting for him to arrive, I recalled I had seen this same hospital room and my dad in that exact same bed before—when I was in heaven.

Pastor Wayne arrived, walked into the room, looked at my dad, and then asked me if I would come out in the hall with him. I followed Pastor Wayne out into the hallway and he said, "I don't think I am supposed to pray for your father's healing. I believe I am supposed to do a sinner's prayer with him."

I was kind of hurt at first because I saw so many people who were very ill get healed when Pastor Wayne prayed for them, but I also knew he was led by the Spirit as to what to do, so I agreed. But I told Pastor Wayne, "My dad is in a coma; how are you going to do a sinner's prayer for him when he doesn't even know you are there?"

Pastor Wayne said, "Don't worry about it. God will work something out." With that, we walked back into the room. Pastor Wayne went over to my dad's right side and took hold of my father's hand like you would in a handshake and said, "Mr. Tuttle, I'm Pastor Wayne Friedt and I am going to say a prayer with you."

I can remember this as clear as if it happened ten seconds ago. My father opened his eyes slightly, barely tilted his head up, and said, "I've been waiting for you."

With that, Pastor Wayne said a prayer, my dad mumbled it after him, and after Pastor Wayne said, "Amen," my father went right back into his coma. Pastor Wayne left right after that, and my dad passed away within seconds.

Praise God my father was able to say this prayer before he died. It's not the way it should be done, so close to death, but I had witnessed my father's salvation years before when I spent that short time in heaven. Although at that time I didn't understand why everything happened like it did, I now know when it is my time to go to heaven and stay there, that I will be greeted by my father and my oldest sister.

CHAPTER 13

OUR EARTH FROM THE BEGINNING

WHILE IN HEAVEN, THE ANGEL TOLD ME to turn and look, and as I turned I saw the earth. It was like it was in a timeline, from the beginning to way into the future. I saw the earth being formed. It looked like a ball of water—no clouds and no land. It was very dark, but I was able to see everything because it was my spirit and not my physical eyes.

The darkness was so powerful and overwhelming, yet I could see all the planets. Then I saw the Spirit of God surround the earth and everything glowed. The Spirit of God is the brightest light you will ever see—makes the sun seem like a shadow. What I saw was that as the Spirit of God hovered over the earth, which was nothing but water, I could see the water glowing, absorbing and reflecting the Spirit of God! The Spirit of God hovered over the earth for a long time, then it lifted up off the earth.

I watched as God said, "Let there be light," and our sun was born.

Next, I saw how God started turning the earth and by doing that separated day from night. Then I saw as the earth received its atmosphere when the waters of the deep separated from the sky. What happened next was very turbulent as the water and the land separated. There it was, one big land mass surrounded by water. The land just came up out of the water, it was all one solid continent, not like we see the earth today.

Watching the land become covered with vegetation, trees, and bushes just by God speaking was powerful! Imagine seeing a desolate place, like a desert or huge rock, and then plants and trees just rise up out of it and the trees that are fruit-bearing already have fruit on them. I don't think CGI could ever come close to what I witnessed.

Then the most beautiful thing happened— God spoke and all the stars lit up in the sky and our moon was formed and brightened up the earth at night. This was the ultimate light show of light shows; nothing I could say could ever fully describe it! As I was allowed to see both day and night on the earth, it was much different than today. At night you could still see almost everything.

The waters of the earth were empty, and then God spoke, and it was filled with life. Fish and other sea dwelling animals appeared. And then, birds just filled the air, millions upon millions of them. They flew over the earth and landed in branches of trees, on the land and sea. Birds started singing so loudly the praises of God!

What happened next was very exciting as different types of animals just started appearing on earth. Every animal you have ever heard about on earth was there. Even what we call livestock, such as cows, goats, sheep, etc. I could go into great detail here, but if you read Genesis 1, you will get the idea of what I saw up to this point.

Now for the part I was most excited and thrilled to watch—I watched God form man! He made man out of the dust or dirt of the earth. God actually used His hands to pick up and form man, unlike all the other things made on earth by just speaking. God made man Himself. He formed man to look like Him and His Son, Jesus.

There was man (Adam), and he stood there lifeless with everything he needed to live on earth—heart, lungs, kidneys, a brain, etc.—but no life flowing through his body. Then God reached down and put His hand behind man's head and put His mouth up to his nostrils, not man's mouth, and He breathed life and Spirit into man!

Man became alive and his whole system worked perfectly. Adam could not only breathe in air, but he could talk with a known language—the language of heaven that every creature on earth knew. All creation could communicate with one language or just by thought. That is how Adam was able to communicate to all the animals, birds, fish, etc. and tell them what they are by name.

Adam was a perfectly made man except he had no belly button. God forbade Adam and Eve to eat from the tree of the knowledge of good and evil, not from the tree of life. God made Adam and Eve to last forever; they never needed to eat from the tree of life. Notice also that if they ate from the tree of knowledge of good and evil they would die. Why did God say that to them? Because God knew He would have to kick them out of the Garden because they would have knowledge to do things other than what God created them to do. Therefore, they would no longer be able to communicate with God in purity and innocence, the way they were created to be.

Now satan, or the serpent, knew that they wouldn't just drop dead from eating that fruit, so when he tempted Eve he made sure he told her that she surely wouldn't die. Yet we all know what happened, and after they both ate of the tree, Adam and Even began to die. Their bodies started to age for the first time. Adam only lived nine hundred and thirty years from that day.

It wasn't until they ate of that fruit that they began to die. Now this brings me to another question I'm sure many have wondered—how long were Adam and Eve in the Garden of Eden? What if I told you that it could have been millions or billions of years; could you accept that or understand that? What if I told you they had many children and those children had children and so on; would you understand or believe that? I have biblical proof.

If you read Genesis 4:1-16 you will see what happened when Cain was born and what happened to him after he killed his brother Abel. Right after Cain killed Abel, the Lord spoke to Cain asking him where his brother was and most of us know his famously quoted answer, "I do not know; am I my brother's keeper?"

God knew Cain was lying and God decided to punish Cain for what he did. Now if you notice when you read Cain's answer in the scriptures, he asked God not to send him away from where he lived, otherwise anyone who found him would kill him. You ever wonder who all those other people where?

All those other people of the earth were once close friends and relatives of Cain. They were the other people who were kicked out of the Garden of Eden along with Adam and Eve. Adam and Eve stayed close to the Garden, but most of the others left and went as far away from Adam and Eve as they could because they were all mad at them for eating from that fruit. Cain and Abel were born after they were kicked out of the Garden.

You need to understand, this is not some new theology; this was part of what I saw from heaven. I am not trying to rewrite the Bible or give you my view. I'm just telling you what I saw when the angel told me to look and see. There is so much more that I saw, but it's impossible to tell you everything in one book.

In fact, I could write ten thousand books and still never cover everything I saw.

I watched as many things from the Old Testament unfolded before my eyes. I saw the tower of Babel and the city they were building. It was amazing to see how everyone on earth not only spoke the same language but how they communicated with each other and animals. Seeing all of them get struck down with different types of language and the confusion afterward was such chaos. No one could speak to each other unless they found others who knew their new language. It confused their way of thinking as each group had to find others who spoke their language. Even their thinking abilities were changed; no longer could they understand the things of high knowledge that they had before. It was difficult enough to just speak or think to do normal things to stay alive. They all lost their ability to communicate with animals as well.

When David killed Goliath, it was much bigger and more supernatural than even the Bible tells. David was maybe five feet one inch tall and Goliath was approximately nine feet tall. David was a ruddy boy, not yet a man, but he had something inside him that we all need today—he had no fear! As he stood there in front of Goliath, he knew that he could beat him. He knew that this giant was flesh and blood and David knew he could kill him. I watched as that sling flung around. It swirled around and around with such speed, and when David let go of the one end to allow the rock to come out, that rock flew directly between the eyes of Goliath. Goliath did not fall for a few moments. He stood there completely stunned; you could tell the pain was intense, and then he crumpled and fell to the ground.

The people around Goliath were screaming at him to get up. They did not know that he was dead immediately. Once they all realized that David had killed Goliath, the Philistines began to run away from the Israelites as they were afraid of their God and the power they possess! They could not get away and hand over everything the Israelites wanted fast enough. Saul was happy and celebrated with everyone, but he became very jealous of David. You can read about this incident in the Bible.

There was so much more, but now I want to take you into the New Testament times and the things I witnessed and saw there.

Let's start with watching Jesus as He went into His ministry. There were possibly millions of miracles that were never recorded. Everything Jesus touched was changed, and when He spoke His words had such power! I watched as He healed many people, and I saw the compassion in His eyes and how He looked and acted toward people. How much He genuinely cared about those around Him. Jesus was a deeply passionate man, and with just one look at you, you would feel His love.

One day Jesus spoke to thousands of people who followed Him around all day long, and whenever Jesus stopped He took time out to talk with them or to show them something. Jesus would feed the crowds by sending a few of His disciples to go buy some food from different places. Jesus also had some people following Him who would cook some food, especially bread, for Him and bring it with them to feed Jesus, His disciples, and the people. I am writing about this because it is not something we think about in today's society, but back then there were no grocery stores or restaurants like today. Many people dedicated themselves to serve Jesus.

I saw Jesus as He walked around, spoke to thousands of people in just one day, and from early evening on He laid hands on thousands of people until early morning. Jesus did not sleep or take breaks. He stayed all night long until all were healed! Many of His disciples and other followers and helpers had to take breaks and sleep, but Jesus never did until the early morning when He was done. Jesus would go and find a place with shade and sleep for a few hours, get up, eat, and then repeat the process all over again. That's how much He loved us and how much compassion He had!

When Jesus spoke to His disciples in private, He wanted so badly for them to understand everything He did. His love for His disciples was very apparent. When one of His disciples understood something that Jesus was teaching them, Jesus would honor that disciple by recognizing him in some way. He handpicked each disciple because He knew what each one was going to do after He left the earth. That was not something that was shown to me; it was just something I understood as I watched Jesus with His disciples.

Jesus cast out more demons than was ever recorded. When Jesus would show up, the demons would cry out from within the people, "Son of Man, what do You want from us?" They did not like Jesus being around, and they recognized who He was. Not because of what He looked like, but because the glory of God was on Him so strong that the demons could feel it whenever He came around. Jesus was God in the flesh! No man has ever had the glory present on him like Jesus had on Him, not even Peter.

Speaking of Peter, I can tell you that his walk with Jesus was unlike all the others. Peter listened to everything Jesus said and wanted to soak in everything he could. Peter couldn't wait to try new things out that Jesus talked about. He was like a little kid, just waiting for Jesus to say or do something—Peter could not wait to go do it himself! I loved watching Peter because he reminded me of myself in some of his ways—childlike!

I won't go into great detail, but I watched as glory was all over Peter as he went through crowds healing the sick. Peter was actually very intense when he was doing God's work, but in private he had a sense of humor. People got healed as Peter's shadow fell on them and not just when he was out and about speaking and praying for the sick, but even when he just walked down streets or pathways.

I watched as they crucified Jesus, and it was not like many would expect. It was much worse. The way they got the crowds to turn on Jesus was so remarkable. Many of these people were healed by Him, and yet when some of the people started yelling to let Barabbas go, the crowd joined in and those who wanted Jesus to be let go were overpowered. It was like it was a well-planned event, much like the protests and violence we have seen in America in 2020. One person gets very loud and is supported by a few other very loud people, and before you know it they develop a crowd mentality to destroy!

When Jesus was whipped, He never yelled, but He did wince and grit His teeth. He took every lash as it ripped His skin apart, like a no one else could ever do. You know it hurt Him—His faced showed it, but not once did He whimper or curse or cry out in pain! I cringed as they drove the spike into His feet and again as they drove the spikes into both His hands. I can't tell you how painful that looked or how horrible it made me feel watching it happen.

Then as they lifted Jesus and His cross up and let it fall into the hole in the ground, it shook His body violently as the cross pounded into place. What struck me was that the guards standing around watching seemed to find pleasure in that. Some people who were allowed to get closer cried when they saw it, but not the guards.

I saw Jesus as He rose up from the dead, back into His human body. I watched Him as He revealed Himself to His disciples. You see, His resurrected body did not look exactly like His body before He died. There were distinct differences. Remember, His body was wrapped up and He suffered great blood loss, and those two things can change your appearance a lot. One thing that really gave away His identity was His eyes. The compassion in them was the same. Jesus really cares about all of us and His heart breaks for those who walk away from Him.

CHAPTER 14

FUTURE EVENTS

MANY OF THE THINGS I WILL TELL YOU are already in the Bible. If you read it, it will confirm what I am saying. There are many things I was shown in heaven about the future of the earth and some things I am not allowed to discuss with you or anyone. If God tells someone to seal it up and not talk about what He has shown you, then you obey, even John in Revelation was not allowed to talk about some things he saw.

Let's talk about the earthquakes I saw while in heaven. Not only will earthquakes happen where they have always happened, but there are going to be great eruptions in the earth where it has lain dormant for hundreds and thousands of years. Not only earthquakes, but volcanic action as well and in areas not expected. Some of these volcanos will be so great that they will tear apart whole areas of a country. Earthquakes so strong that no one has ever recorded one like it in modern times. A 9.5 to 12.5 will be recorded in the future.

Asia will suffer in many ways it has not suffered before. Not only will buildings come down, but whole large cities will be flattened by earthquakes. Many people will die by being crushed to death by the force of these earthquakes—those are the unlucky ones. The people who will suffocate after weeks of being buried alive are the ones who will have a chance to accept Jesus as their Lord before they die, but their suffering will be great. The Asian continent, mostly China, will have strange things happen to it, almost like plagues, and all the fish will die in a lake and no one will ever find out what caused it, and rivers will turn blood red overnight.

I wrote about the things mentioned above in 2013, and China has already experienced some of these things now in 2020. We have had the coronavirus—it's like a plague, and all the fish have died in lakes and no one has discovered why. There have been two rivers that have turned blood red overnight so far.

Furthermore, people will get sores inside their mouths and doctors will not be able to cure them. The cancer rate will climb drastically, while in other countries the progression of cancer will slow down. Children will be born with unusual birth defects and the doctors will not know what causes them. There will be born a few blonde-haired children to a few Asian couples, and no one will be able to explain why. While in South Korea in 2015, I saw a young man who was from China—he had almost white-blond hair and very light-colored eyes. Both of his parents are Chinese and there is no other race involved.

Coming soon, there will be a great collapse of currency in China and it will affect the whole world, but it will affect all of Asia the most. This will happen as you see businesses leave China and whole countries will condemn China. Watch as car manufactures start leaving China. Germany will be the key to when this will happen as they will leave, and China collapses.

Europe will have more than its fair share of disasters too. Earthquakes will destroy places that have been around for centuries and these earthquakes will be located where some have never been before. Many livestock will die of strange diseases and plague-like infections that can't be controlled by antibiotics. Dams and bridges will be destroyed by earthquakes and floods. There will be times of extreme drought and then extreme rains that seem to never stop raining, sometimes for forty-five days straight. European countries will start to not trust the other European countries and they will withdraw from each other.

I saw these things in 1978 and wrote the above in 2013, and everyone was doing fine with each other then. Now we have had Brexit, and very soon other countries will pull away from the European Union. Italy and Spain as well as Poland are uneasy with the EU and that split will get deeper as time goes on. Natural disasters will happen throughout all Europe.

Russia will suffer in different ways; there will be things that happen over the skies of Russia that will make people repent because they are so unusual. Not only will the earth shake in Russia, but it will open up holes in places, unusual types never seen before.

There have been holes opening up in Russia now. In 2013 when I wrote this, there were no holes like this in Russia or anyplace else in the world. My first copy of this book came out on April 1, 2014, and in July of 2014 scientists in Russia started finding these huge holes in Siberia. Some holes measure over 200 feet across. There has even been a TV show called *What on Earth* that examined these holes, and so far no one can tell exactly what caused them. The name of the place these holes are found is called "The End of the World" by the locals.

Russia will become boastful for a time, seeming to be the big bear again, but that will collapse because the people will not want to be ruled like that again. The Russian people are proud, they take pride in their ways, but they no longer want war; they want to live in peace. They are good people and they have learned to live with hardships and live a difficult life compared to most other standards of the world, and they have not only survived but have proven they are a strong people.

Sweden, Norway, and Denmark have always been a place of refuge, but not in the coming years. They will see disasters they have never dealt with before. Some of their own people will start to commit horrendous crimes like they have never seen, and families will turn against families. War will break out between them and other parts of the world. They will no longer be a safe haven.

South America will see some of the worst earthquakes and the most frequent for a time. Usually the earthquakes are related to the western half, but the eastern side will have some as well now. Countries like Ecuador, Columbia, and Chile will be a hot spot for earthquakes. Crime in Brazil will climb higher than ever before; there will be violence in the country of Brazil like it has never seen before. In the jungles and rainforests, there will be fires that seem like they will never stop. In Rio de Janeiro you will see buildings and large statues that will fall as the earth continues to shift.

Several things are already coming to pass since I wrote the above. Crime in Brazil has climbed to an all-time high. The violence and deaths are climbing daily. The rainforest has seen fires that burn out of control where hundreds of square miles are burnt up.

India will suffer greatly as the earth shakes and rattles all who live there. No one in India or Pakistan will escape from this terror. Some will die from this, others from starvation, and yet others from robbers and looters. The women will be raped and ravished, forced into horrible situations such as sex slaves—this includes girls as young as six years old. This not only happens in India but parts of

Indonesia too. The plagues caused by the dead bodies lying in the alleyways and in the streets will kill thousands upon thousands in that part of the world. There will be no food for almost half of India and Pakistan in those days.

What is so sad is that part of what I saw from heaven has already occurred since writing this. Many women are being forced into being sex slaves, and young girls at the age of six are being raped and forced into sex slavery. There were reports that on April 30, 2018, a six-year-old girl was raped. It was in the news.

Africa will become divided between Christians and non-Christians, and there will be horrible wars. The people of the Muslim faith will try to kill all Christians in that area because they feel they must rule all of Africa. They fill people's heads with lies about a better afterlife and they promise them things they cannot deliver. By the time they find out they have been tricked or fooled, it is too late. The stench from dying bodies there will be horrible. Diseases will run rampant in all of Africa, and because of their sinful desires the diseases will spread even faster than anyone could have expected. Men, women, and children alike will be infected and die.

Mexico and Central America will suffer much like South America, except there will be a good-sized volcano to erupt in Mexico. The earthquakes in Mexico will kill more because of landslides caused by the earthquakes and the volcano erupting. People will die from starvation in parts of northern and central Mexico. People in Central America and Mexico will have diseases that give flu-like symptoms, but the fevers will be over 105 degrees and the people will die, especially children.

North America, including the United States and Canada, will receive its fair share of earthquakes and volcanoes erupting. There will be a massive volcano eruption in the United States that will affect the whole world's climate, and this was not something expected. The volcano will erupt out of Wyoming, in the Yellowstone area, and it will be so massive that for hundreds of miles around nothing will be left standing and the toxic cloud it will produce and the ash cloud will cover most of Canada and two thirds of the United States. It will change the global climate and even people in the tropics will feel freezing temperatures for the first time.

This volcano was shown to me in 1978, way before scientists were publishing anything about Yellowstone. I want you to know that this will not be something expected; they will expect a much lesser up-push of the earth, but their expectations will be totally miscalculated when the big explosion happens. A sign will be when the big geysers in Yellowstone erupt with unusual timing as some, like Old Faithful, will stop for days on end. To give a little comfort to those reading this, I didn't see this happening in the near future.

This is not all that will happen. The sin and corruption that has been so blatant will increase until the time that God has set aside for the people to revolt as one. As we all know now, this revolt started in 2016 when we elected Donald J. Trump to be our President. There is much more to come! When this time comes there will be a major shift in how this government is run. The people will take back their governments and the liberal policies will be overturned. God will be put back into their government and schools. Finally, in January of 2020, President Trump moved to protect prayer in schools, and he set up federal funds for religious organizations!

Let me tell you about something else I saw here in North America. Did you know that all the Native Americans, or First Nations, all loved God and worshiped Him at one time? Did you know that they also knew about Jesus, the Son of God? It was beautiful back then in our country as all worshiped God! It wasn't until one man became so jealous of God that he started making his own magic to fool people. Soon he wanted to be worshiped by the people.

This started with one man and then spread to other nations and tribes. Soon everyone had their own medicine man or shaman. As the medicine man or shaman popularity grew, they started finding ways to get people high off of different plants. Soon they discovered hallucinogenic plants that would allow them and others to have what they called a spiritual experience. Unfortunately, this has taken over most of these First Nations people, but God showed me that a huge revival is coming to them!

Australia and New Zealand will not be spared by the earthquakes and natural disasters. New Zealand will get hit especially hard on the number of earthquakes, but it will not see the 9.5 or higher earthquakes. It will have many of them, though. Australia will suffer more by weather-related occurrences than anything else. The extreme heat and cold will grip that nation and there will be pestilence over that country that has never been seen before. Flies and gnats will fill the air and make the skies seem dark during the day.

We now know that Australia has been experiencing, over the last couple of years, some of the strangest weather they have ever faced— heat waves and droughts that seemed like they would not end. They have been plagued with flies and gnats to the point they were getting into everything including their eyes, noses, mouths, etc. Let's not forget the wildfires that have ravaged Australia either. New Zealand has been seeing more than its fair shares of earthquakes as well since this book was first published in 2013.

There is a sound like no other sound heard before on earth that people from every nation will hear—it is the sound of the earth moaning. This sound will travel all around the earth and people will hear it and try to explain it. They will even record it, but no one can explain what it really is and where it came from, but you will know it is the earth moaning!

This sound has already started now. It has been heard in Russia, Norway, Sweden, the United Kingdom, Africa, Europe, Asia, the Middle East, South America, Central America, Australia, India, and many more countries. I know that in the winter of 2016, while living in Spokane, Washington, I heard the sound personally and so did everyone else from over a 75-mile radius. It was on all the local news stations and it sounded almost like a huge snowplow was scraping through deep ice and snow and scraping the pavement at the same time. They could never find the source of that sound.

No nation, no continent, no state, and no city will escape this wrath. The earth will seem to turn on itself and cause many to believe the end is near, but these things must happen. Some of you reading this book will see these things occur, while some will just see the beginning of it. The warning light is on, the siren is sounding. Take heed and be warned, pray. These things can be changed through prayer, just as Moses changed God's mind not to kill the Israelites, so you can change the course of events through prayer, but some natural disasters will have to happen because not everyone will take the warnings and they will battle against God.

Now this is what happens because of these things. People will turn their backs on the ways in which sin was ruling their life; they will know that there is a God. Yes, there will be wars and rumors of wars, but there will be peace among those who believe. Those who really love the Lord will not feel abandoned but will feel the love God has for them.

CHAPTER 15

FINAL WORDS

I F YOU HAVE READ THIS FAR THEN I THINK it's only fair I explain a few more things to you. I am a Spirit-filled Christian; I believe in all the gifts of the Spirit. I believe that people can get healed by the power of God, that the lame can walk and the blind can see, that demonic powers can be cast out or off of a person, and I believe in the full gospel of Jesus Christ. I believe in miracles, and yes, they happen today. I also believe that we have not even begun to scratch the surface of what God is going to release here on earth, and the Great

Outpouring of the Holy Spirit has not yet appeared in its fullness. That is still to come.

I know for a fact that there are things that will be coming that have not happened yet and that are going to be greater than anything that has ever been seen on earth. I also know that 2014 was a year when some special gifts and an extraordinary outpouring began here on earth. In 2017, God started releasing things in the government that will change this country and the world forever. There will be signs in the heavens and on earth. These are warnings that you must repent, turn away from your old ways, and seek the face of God. I know that in 2016, beginning in August, there was another type of spiritual gift that was poured out among His people.

Late in 2020, there will begin a great outpouring like has never been seen on the earth before. God's glory will start to fall on people and revivals will start to break out throughout the world, starting in the United States! These revivals will be spontaneous. They will not be named after a person or place because they will start to happen in different areas around the Unites States and spread to every nation on earth. But this will not happen because of man; it will happen because it is the time that God has set aside for His glory to fall on earth.

There will be people who don't even know who Jesus is and they will fall on their face and cry out for forgiveness without anyone else around speaking to them about God or Jesus. People will be filled with the Holy Spirit and start speaking in tongues and even perform miracles because God's glory will be all over them! This will be a time when God will allow the glory to be on earth like it was when Peter's shadow fell on people and they were healed!

There will be manifestations in the Spirit that have never been shown to man before, but we also must be aware of false prophets. The false prophets will be known by their greed, not just for money, but their greed for everyone to believe and follow them. Be smart, stay in the Bible, pray daily to God, be filled with the Holy Spirit, and read His Word and seek Him daily. Reading the Bible daily does not get you to heaven—accepting Jesus as your Lord and Savior does that—but reading His Word gives you strength and allows your spirit to grow in the ways of the Lord and it will give you wisdom—godly wisdom.

As I explained in earlier chapters, our minds can't fathom what the spirit can, and being prayed up and having the knowledge God gave us to study in His Word gives us good judgment and understanding. There is much more for you to read than the few words I have written in this book You can have a real, personal relationship with Jesus. There are so many more things in store for you if you will just seek Him and ask Him. Read God's Word and you will soon understand that there is much more for you than just reading His Word and praying, but that is where it starts.

I am not pushing any religion on you; I am just trying to help you perceive that there is more to life and death than what we can know with our minds and that God loves everyone. He sent His Son to die for us so that we might be able to go to heaven. What I am attempting to do is help you so you can look in your Bible and see that what I am talking about is already there in your Bible. Look in the book of Acts. In the world today, with all the demonic activity, you need everything heaven can give you. So take advantage of it while you can, because after you die it will be too late.

This is the time when we will all start seeing the Spirit of the Lord sweep across the earth. It's not going to be limited to here in the U.S. It is going to move through China, India, Europe, Canada, England, Australia, New Zealand, South America, Japan, Thailand, all of Asia, Mexico, Africa, and all around the entire globe. China will experience one of the biggest explosions of the Holy Spirit—even some of those in the government are going to accept Jesus and receive the Holy Spirit! There are going to be small villages in China that have been pretty much unheard of before, and everyone in those villages will be saved and filled with the Holy Spirit. Even people in Tibet will be filled with the Spirit!

While I was in heaven, I was given these dates and others and was told not to release anything till I was given the okay by the Spirit. I have kept all this information and more since 1978. I didn't have any idea what I was going to grow up to be like or what life was even going to be like when I got older, but I had to keep quiet until now. Part of the reason for that is because the world would not have been ready for it before; there had to be a couple different moves by the Holy Spirit before people would understand these things, and even so there are still going to be those who don't believe,; but that is their chance they take.

The Lord is going to pour His Spirit out over the world like never before. There are going to be things happening that will shake up many churches. Some churches are going to come up against this move of the Spirit; some churches will embrace it. Most importantly, there are going to be people with no real church association who are going to not only accept it but move in it as well. This great outpouring of the Holy Spirit is not going to be limited to the churches. There will be people all over the world who have never heard about the Holy Spirit before, who will get saved and filled with the Holy Spirit, and immediately will start performing miracles through the power of the Holy Spirit. They will lay hands on the sick and they will recover. They will cast out demonic spirits in Jesus' name because the Spirit has given them power to do these things.

There are going to be people who aren't Christians at all who will be sitting in their own home watching TV or on their computer and the convicting power of the Holy Spirit will fall on them. They will give their hearts to the Lord, accept Jesus, and be filled with the Holy Spirit even though they know nothing about Jesus or the Holy Spirit except that someone mentioned Jesus before to them. Again, this is not limited to the United States. This will be happening globally in every nation around the world. The Holy Spirit will be moving upon these people to convict them of their sins. It will not come from hearing a preacher or even someone witnessing to them. It will just be part of the great outpouring of the Holy Spirit, the global glory!

If you understand things of a spiritual nature, then the things I am talking about will make perfect sense to you. There are many more things that were revealed to me, and sometime soon I will be writing more about them, but in the meantime take heed what the Spirit of God has revealed. Those of you with hidden intentional sin need to get on your face before the Lord and repent, which means to not only ask for forgiveness but to change your ways. The warning about hidden intentional sin is a very stern warning and it has been given in order to save your life, not to embarrass you nor condemn you. God does not want your sin to be revealed to everyone. He just wants you to repent, in private if necessary, and change your lifestyle. God loves you!

I am not perfect. I have done things in my life I am ashamed of, I have sinned, and I have had hidden intentional sin in my life. I broke the law years ago, and I am totally unworthy to write this book except that I have been for-given, cleansed, and sanctified through the blood of Jesus. I am a servant of Christ and only justified through Christ to be an author-ity on what I have been through. If it wasn't for my mother praying for me all these years, I don't believe I would be here today to write this book; it would have been a much worse ending. Thank you, Mother, thank you so much!

> *I pray that, having read these things in this book, if you need help with repentance the Holy Spirit will help you. I pray that each and every one of you who has not accepted Jesus as your personal Savior will accept Him now and have the understand-ing that Jesus died on the cross to forgive you of your sins. I also pray that you seek more about the Lord and the Holy Spirit as you finish reading this book but, most of all, that you give your life to Jesus. All these things are gifts from God to*

anyone who asks, so I pray that you do ask God to do these things for you today.

Now would be a good time in your life to get another book that is much better than this one—it's called the Bible—and start reading it every day.

IF YOU WANT TO MAKE SURE YOU'RE GOING TO HEAVEN

Here is a simple prayer you can say out loud right now if you have not accepted Jesus into your heart.

Lord Jesus, I come before You today asking that You forgive me of my sins. I accept You, Jesus, into my heart. I know You died on the cross to forgive me of my sins and You rose from the grave and are seated at the right hand of Your Father. I repent of my sins, I will turn away from the things I have been doing wrong. I thank You, Lord, for coming into my heart now. I know now that Your Spirit dwells in me. I make You Lord and Savior over my life. In Jesus' name I pray, amen.

It's that simple; now you are a child of the King!

IF YOU FEEL LIKE YOU'RE UNSURE

If you feel like your salvation is in question and want to know for sure, then just repeat this prayer out loud, right where you are.

Father God, forgive me for walking away from You. I repent right now, Lord, and ask Jesus back into my life. Forgive me for the wrong I have done. Now I thank You, God, for accepting me back, and this time I will do everything I can not to stray from You. Thank You, God, for forgiving me. I look forward to having a great relationship with You. In Jesus' name I pray, amen.

FINAL THOUGHTS

I leave you with this final thought—don't fall for the entrapment that the devil has laid out for you. The deceptions come in many forms, but trust me—if it feels just slightly wrong, it is wrong. Sinning and backsliding doesn't just happen overnight; it starts as something very small—a thought, a glance at something you shouldn't look at, a word, a dirty joke you laugh at, whatever it is that is just the beginning. If you resist it then—the thought, the glance, the joke, etc.—it has to flee; it will not grow, and you will not fail or backslide. However, if you allow that thought, that glance, that joke to grow, then you will fail, and you will backslide. Pastor Wayne Friedt used to say something every Sunday morning years ago from the pulpit. He said, "What you feed grows and what you starve dies." That goes for the physical, mental, and spiritual, so starve out those bad thoughts and negative things in life and feed yourself positive and godly things. Then the actions of your life will bear godly fruit, and you will not fall for the trap satan has waiting for you!

ABOUT IVAN TUTTLE

Ivan S. Tuttle has been a business owner, vice president of a large corporation, a manager, and an ordained minister. He has served the Lord for many years and his proudest accomplishment is speaking at churches around the country about his death experience and seeing people turn their lives over to the Lord.